GIRLS AND ATHLETICS

This edition published by Lector House in 2024

ISBN: 978-93-6138-034-1
Edition copyright © 2024 by Lector House LLP
All rights reserved under the International Copyright Conventions.

Every possible effort has been made to ensure that the information contained in this book is accurate at the time of going to press and the publisher cannot accept responsibility for any errors or omissions, however caused, in this unabridged, slightly corrected republication of the text of the first edition. No responsibility for loss or damage occasioned to any person, acting or refraining from action, as a result of the material in this publication can be accepted by the publisher. The publisher is not associated with any product or vendor mentioned in the book. The contents of this work are intended to further general scientific research, understanding and discussion, only. Readers should consult with a specialist, where appropriate.

No part of this publication may be reproduced, stored in a retrieval system, or transmitted, in any form, or by any means, electronic, mechanical, photocopying or otherwise, without the prior permission of the publisher.

Lector House LLP
Registered Office: H. No. 96, Block C, Tomar Colony,
Burari, Delhi – 110084, India
info@lectorhouse.com
www.lectorhouse.com

GIRLS AND ATHLETICS

MARY C. MORGAN

2024

LECTOR HOUSE LLP

MARY C. MORGAN.

GIRLS AND ATHLETICS

GIVING A BRIEF SUMMARY OF THE ACTIVITY, RULES AND METHOD OF ADMINISTRATION OF THE FOLLOWING GAMES IN GIRLS' SCHOOLS AND COLLEGES, WOMEN'S CLUBS, ETC.

ARCHERY, BASKET BALL, CRICKET, FENCING, FIELD DAY, FIELD HOCKEY, GYMNASTICS, GOLF, HAND BALL, ICE HOCKEY, INDOOR BASE BALL, ROWING, SOCCER, SKATING, SWIMMING, TENNIS, TRACK ATHLETICS, VOLLEY BALL, WALKING, WATER POLO, WATER BASKET BALL

EDITED BY

MARY C. MORGAN

of Lansdowne Country Club Philadelphia

(A Member of the Class of 1915, Bryn Mawr College)

PUBLISHERS' NOTE

Miss Mary C. Morgan, who has been chosen to edit the volume, "*Girls and Athletics*" is an all-around athlete of remarkable ability. As a student at Friends Central School, Philadelphia, and at Bryn Mawr College Miss Morgan played on basket ball, track, water polo, and field hockey teams and participated in the gymnastic events. At Bryn Mawr she held the individual cup in 1913 and 1914 for the highest number of points in the Interclass Track and Field meet. On the track she shares the world's record for women of 12 seconds in the 100-yard dash and she holds the world's record of 15-2/5 seconds in the 100-yard hurdle race of eight hurdles each 2 feet 6 inches high. Both of these records were made on cinder track with rubber-soled shoes in the cumbersome bloomer and jumper costume (cumbersome as compared to the scanty attire of male track and field athletes). Miss Morgan also shares the Bryn Mawr College record of 6-1/5 seconds for the 50-yard dash and holds the college record for the standing broad jump—7 feet 9 inches.

AMERICAN SPORTS PUBLISHING CO.

ACKNOWLEDGMENTS

The editor is very much indebted to the following persons for their kind interest and assistance: Miss Harriet Ballintine, Director of Physical Training at Vassar College; Mr. Philip Bishop, Instructor in Gymnastics at the Haverford School and Advisory Swimming Coach at Bryn Mawr College; Dr. Frances Boynton of the New Haven Normal School of Physical Training; Miss Elizabeth Burchenal, Executive Secretary of the Girls' Branch of the Public Schools Athletic League, New York, and to the committee of the League: Dr. Florence Gilman of Smith College; Miss Josephine Katzenstein, a member of the Lansdowne Country Club and the All-Philadelphia Hockey teams; Miss Lorena L. Parrish, Physical Director of Howard Payne College; Miss Lillian Schoedler, Honorary President of the Intercollegiate Alumnæ Athletic League; Miss Dorothy Wooster of Smith College, and Mr. A. M. Gillam.

The editor also wishes to thank the schools, colleges and country clubs who so kindly replied to the *questionaire* sent out.

BIBLIOGRAPHY

Spalding's Official Athletic Handbooks (American Sports Publishing Company, New York).

Official Handbook of the Girls' Branch of the Public Schools Athletic League, New York. Handbook of Athletic Games (Bancroft and Pulvermacher; Macmillan, New York). A Survey of Track Athletics for Women (Reprinted from the American Physical Education Review, January, 1916). Dr. Harry E. Stewart, Physical Director New Haven (Conn.) Normal School of Gymnastics.

CONTENTS

GIRLS AND ATHLETICS

BY MARY C. MORGAN

In gathering information for this volume a *questionaire* was sent to some three hundred schools and colleges. Replies were received from two hundred and thirty-seven of these. Of this number only one school went on record as opposed to athletics for girls and women. All of the others make provision for athletics or some form of physical education. Some schools provide little or no supervision, it is true, but the great majority provide for or realize the necessity for provision of adequate control of this form of training.

The impression one receives from scanning the replies to the *questionaire* is undoubtedly that general athletics for girls are becoming more and more popular, and that development is slowly but surely broadening out to include eventually almost every form of athletics for almost every girl.

From the physical standpoint, any exercise under favorable circumstances is beneficial in that it develops and brings into play the muscles of the body and stimulates the whole system. But all forms of athletics should be carefully supervised, particularly for growing girls. Every participant should have a thorough physical examination and if any limitations are placed upon her athletics, the reasons for such restrictions should be carefully explained. It is natural that some people are more delicate than others—absolutely unfit for some of the more strenuous games—but there are always less strenuous exercises which may be indulged in.

The physical condition being assured, the girl should be watched so that she does not enter into the sports or games with too much intensity. It is a common tendency of the average American girl to throw her whole soul into the particular matter at hand. If it happens to be athletics, often her enthusiasm helped out by a thoroughly admirable spirit and by quite a lot of "grit"—as her brothers term it—keeps her playing when she is really tired out physically. This is the time where a coach—or if there is no coach, friendly advice—will show the girl that she is not getting any benefit out of the exercise, and she is running the risk of injuring herself.

This excess is as wrong in athletics as it is in anything else. Be temperate.

My advice to every girl is: Know your physical condition; use common sense and gauge the amount of exercise you take by your physical condition and stamina.

Athletics as a builder of character *are* just as important as a builder of physical strength. *Fair play* and *good sportsmanship* are the two maxims kept constantly before the eye. A girl who has won the reputation of being a clean, square player is happy herself and is admired by all with whom she comes in contact. There is no higher compliment than to be called a "good sportswoman." A girl who can lose and smile, or win and not exult over her opponent's defeat, is quite apt to get something bigger than mere physical development out of her athletics.

Training

A few girls have asked me, "How can I learn to play this or that game well?" Athletics are just like almost every phase of life; it requires practice and experience before one becomes skilled. If, then, a girl wishes to be successful it is best to make a thorough study of the branch of sport she is going to take up and practice, assimilating each detail carefully. The amount of time it takes to become proficient depends upon the natural ability of the person—some people are much more talented in athletics than others.

The best advice I can give is to know your game thoroughly, so that you may play with your head as well as your body. Practice until you have confidence in your ability. Do not practice so constantly and continually that you become "stale." A little practice taken regularly is often more beneficial than a lot of practice which tires you out so that you are unfit for more the next day. Do a little bit, so that you are not tired, increasing the practice slowly.

Some people believe in set training rules; others do not. It is best to be in good physical condition all the time if it is possible; it stands to reason, however, that for especial speed and endurance the physical condition should be nearly perfect. Sleep is a very necessary factor; therefore, every athlete should have a long and sound sleep every night. As for diet, there is a difference of opinion. It seems reasonable that no heavy food, nor rich food that is indigestible, should be eaten. In particular, just before a contest, a light meal should be eaten with the proper time for digestion allowed before playing. Some people make the mistake of eating heavily and then playing immediately afterward. The most sensible training seems to be, eat the most nourishing and easily digested food.

What to Wear

Dress sensibly. For track and field games, basket ball and other games that require speed, agility and the freest play of all muscles, by all means wear bloomers and a middy blouse. For tennis, golf and the other less strenuous games, wear shirtwaist or middy blouse and a skirt wide enough and short enough to give the most play of the leg muscles. For instance, there is nothing so ridiculous as to see a girl athlete togged with more regard for the impression she is making on the male part of the gallery than for getting the most physical benefit out of her game. I have great sympathy for every girl who takes pride in her appearance at all times. I maintain that it is both possible to present a neat and an agreeable appearance and at the same time to dress sensibly for the business at hand. In each of the following chapters on the various forms of sports I have endeavored to say a word about dress specifically for that sport, unless it is evident what costume is suitable. Back of it all I will repeat this fundamental: Dress sensibly.

FIELD HOCKEY

The Game; the team as a whole; how to hold stick; passing; dribbling; the bully; shooting goals; positions of team.

The Regulations—Field; goals; striking circle; dress; stick, time, score, officials.

Rules—I., governing bully; II., for goal; III., for sticks; IV., for free hit; for out of bounds; VI., for undercutting; VII., for offside; VIII., running in on the left; IX., turning on the ball; X., handling; XI., kicking; XII., rough play; XIII., time-out; XIV., umpire.

Field hockey, next to basket ball, is the most popular team game played by girls; and it is a comparatively new game here, as it has been played in America only since 1901. Miss Harriet Ballintine, Director of Physical Training at Vassar College, in her pamphlet, "The History of Physical Training at Vassar College," gives an account of the beginning of hockey in America: "Until 1901, English field hockey was comparatively unknown in this country. Before this it had been played by men at the Springfield Training School, and to some extent at Mount Holyoke College. Dr. J. H. McCurdy of the Springfield School in writing of the game says: 'The men at Springfield first played the game of field hockey in 1897. Regarding where field hockey was first played in this country (by girls), the girls at Mount Holyoke College had begun playing the game, I think, before Miss Applebee's arrival in this country. They had been down to a number of our championship games. Arrangements had been made for some of our students to coach the Mount Holyoke girls in hockey, when I found Miss Applebee was in this country and recommended their getting her.'"

Many hockey players owe their interest in the game to Miss Applebee, notable for her inspiring coaching and the knowledge of hockey that she has imparted to her pupils.

To the devotees of this game, there is no other sport that quite comes up to it. In a game of hockey there is a spirit of freedom, of exhilaration, of gladness that comes from a true love of sport. And it has other advantages—absence of roughness, plenty of vigorous exercise in the open air, and yet not extraordinarily violent. It is a game that may be played by all types; a game that is played by a large number on each team.

The Game.

Hockey is played on a level field of turf similar to a football or lacrosse field.

There are eleven players on each team, thus there are twenty-two players on the field at one time. Each player is equipped with a stick with a curved head. A cricket ball is used. The eleven players are divided into groups: forwards, halfbacks, fullbacks and goal. Each group calls for a different type of player. The teams line up (according to illustration) in the center of the field. The forwards are the attackers, whose duty it is to advance the ball into their opponents' territory and score a goal (Rule II). The halfbacks assist the forwards in attacking and with the fullbacks and goal keeper defend their own goal.

The umpire blows the whistle and the game begins with the two center forwards bullying. The ball has been placed in the middle of center line, the center forwards stand with one foot on each side of center line directly opposite each other, right shoulder toward their own goal. (See Rule for Bully.) After the bully is completed, the ball hit out, then play commences. The forwards of the team in possession of the ball rush it down toward the opponents' goal and try to shoot a goal while the opposing defense tries to prevent any score. Each time the ball is fairly hit over the goal line, one point is made by team scoring goal. Two halves, length of which is agreed upon by captains, are played. The team scoring the greatest number of goals by the end of second half wins the game.

The Team as a Whole.

The main factor in hockey is team play. There may be one or two players of stellar ability on the team, but if the team does not play well together it is not well balanced. It is not an individual but eleven individuals welded together that form a team. Every girl should consider—when playing hockey—that her stick is her best friend; therefore it should be chosen carefully and with due consideration. There are three important qualities a stick should have: balance, weight and length. The balance should be even, not in the handle, but more in the curved head of stick; not too heavy there however. The weight of the stick should be 21 or 22 ounces for a forward, 23 or 24 for a halfback, 24 or 25 for a fullback or goal keeper. Never carry a stick that is too heavy. The stick should be just long enough for a comfortable grip. It should be neither too long nor too short.

How to Hold Stick.

The stick should be firmly held in both hands, with the left hand gripping the handle at the end (top) of stick with the fingers forward; the right hand grips the stick directly below the left hand, touching but not overlapping the left hand. The hands should never be separated because this tends to make a player stoop over, thus losing in strength of stroke. At the beginning of the stroke, the stick should be carried back toward the right (the right arm must be kept straight to avoid "sticks"—a foul, see Rule III) until the left arm is straight; then the stick should be carried forward, striking ball squarely. At the finish of the stroke, the right arm should still be kept straight and the end of stick turned in (i.e., toward body) and down to avoid making "sticks" at end of stroke.

While the stick is not in use or while player is running it should be carried in both hands horizontally at comfortable height, as long as it is below the shoulder.

Let us consider the forward line. It is made up of five positions: left wing, left inside, center forward, right inside, right wing. Players for these positions should be selected for the following qualifications: ability to run with average speed; ability to shoot hard, clean goals; endurance and wind necessary for constant sprints. It is up to the forwards to keep the ball in the opponents' territory; for this, there are two ways of advancing the ball—passing and dribbling.

Passing.

Passing, since it is less individual and makes for more team play, should be ranked first. There are short and long passes. The short are generally quick passes between a forward and her nearest teammate, that is, between an inside and center or between an inside and wing. The long pass is across the center from the left side of the field to the right, or *vice versa*. All passes should be quick, clean and accurate. Here are a few things to avoid: Don't pass the ball straight ahead so that it goes to one of opposing team. *Don't pass behind your own forward line.* Don't pass to a guarded player. Don't wait to pass until you have been attacked, thus hurrying your pass. Don't (especially when passing to the wings) put all your strength in the stroke, sending the hardest ball you can.

Dribbling.

Next to passing comes dribbling. Every forward should know how to dribble. In dribbling the ball, both hands should be kept close together at the top of the stick; the stick is sometimes turned so that the flat side is forward; the wrist and hands are adjusted to any position of the stick. Only a few players are skilled enough to dribble with one hand. The ball should be kept close to the stick, slightly in advance of the runner. The most common fault is that the dribbler follows the ball instead of sending the ball just where she desires. The player who is a good dribbler keeps the ball under control, no matter how speedily she is running. If the ball is sent ahead too far then the dribbler is apt to lose control, but if it is kept close to the stick and just barely touched each time it is easier to manage. The dribbler should remember: never crouch over the ball, but stand erect; never let the ball get too far ahead; never permit an opponent to get so close that you cannot pass the ball to a teammate quickly. *Never keep the ball selfishly.*

The Bully.

The forwards are called on frequently to bully—the start and twenty-five-yard bully (see Rule I)—so the bully should be practised until each forward is quick and accurate. There should be an understanding among the forwards and halfbacks as to which way the ball will be hit out on the bully so that some one is always ready for it. The right hand should grip almost three-quarters way down the stick, the player then must bend over the stick. The feet are wide apart, planted firmly on the ground. (See Rule for Bully.) After the three separate "grounds and sticks" the ball is hit out. It is here that quickness and skill count. The halfbacks—one from each team—always back up a bully to help their forwards.

Shooting Goals.

It is not necessary to say that it is most important for a forward to shoot goals. She should shoot as often, as hard and as accurately as she can, and she must follow her shots in. This is her main duty and no forward is up to the mark unless she *can shoot goals.*

Center Forward.

Center forward is the keystone position. Her duties are to bully off at the center (for start and after each goal), to keep the forwards in a straight line, to shoot goals, *to distribute passes to the left and right sides evenly.* If a center forward has a clear field it is all right for her to dribble, but, as a rule, she should play a passing game. *She also has many opportunities to shoot.*

Field Hockey—The bulley-off. The players are in position and the opposing center forwards are in the act of putting the ball in play.

Field Hockey—A corner. The defending team is lined up on the goal line. The attacking forwards are lined up along the striking circle, ready to return the hit and convert it into a goal.

Right Inside.

The right inside is governed by the same dribbling and passing rule as the center. She should be particular to receive the passes of the left wing. Also a lot of the shooting falls to her. Both insides should play close to the center if the center has the ball, or close to the wing if the wing has the ball.

Left Inside.

The left inside is a more difficult position to receive passes and to shoot from. It is often wiser for a left inside to allow a ball to go to another forward if she is not in a good position to receive it. As a rule, the best balls for her are from the right.

Right Wing.

The wings should be fast players. In particular, the right wing has a splendid opportunity for dribbling and passing. It is mainly the duty of the wings to advance the ball; if, however, the opportunity arises, they should shoot. The wing should be careful never to send the ball too far ahead; never to let a ball go outside the side lines if it is possible to stop it; never dribble farther than the twenty-five-yard line; always send the ball toward the center of the field.

Left Wing.

The left wing should be careful to dribble only when she has a clear field. In receiving a ball, the wing, if possible, should stand with her left shoulder toward the goal she is attacking. Three common faults of a left wing are: Letting the ball go out of bounds on her side too often, thus giving the other side a roll-in; getting into an off-side position; turning on the ball. (See Rules VII and IX.)

Halfbacks.

All of the halfback positions are extremely hard to play because they require great endurance, a moderate amount of speed, hard hitting, and a fighting spirit. The halfbacks are both attackers and defenders. First, in attacking they feed the forwards by passes to them. They should follow up the forward line closely and when the forwards are inside the circle should be ready to shoot if a chance comes. On the defensive they should stick to the opposing forwards closely. The fullbacks and halfbacks should work together on defense.

Center Halfback.

The center halfback backs up the bullies in the center of the field and she feeds primarily the center and insides. In defending she guards the opposing center forward and the insides if they are playing close to the center. The half should always watch to see which forwards are free. She should not send the ball to the spot from which it has just come, as that spot is apt to be guarded, but should change the direction.

Right Halfback.

The right halfback feeds the right wing and the right inside. If both of these are carefully guarded, then she should send ball to center or to the other side of field. In defense she guards the left wing or the left inside—if the inside is near the wing. She also backs up all the bullies on her side of the line.

Left Halfback.

The left halfback feeds the left wing and the left inside unless they are guarded, then she changes the direction of the ball. The left half should send very careful, well-placed balls to her wing and inside, balls that slant a little bit, not straight ahead. As the right wing is apt to dribble, the left half should be very quick and should be careful to avoid running in on the left. (Rule VIII.)

The halfbacks should remember: Never to give up; if your opponent gets away, run after her and stop her; never hit through the forward line, always hit the ball to somebody; never run out of position to tackle an opponent. Each half should stick closely to the girl she is guarding. Never interfere with the work of the fullback or the goal keeper.

Fullbacks.

The fullbacks are primarily defensive players although they have opportunities for long shots to the forwards. The fullbacks and the halfbacks should never mix up, by guarding the same girl. The fullbacks stay near their own goal. If the right half is guarding the left wing and the center half the center forward, then the left inside remains for the right fullback to guard. When one fullback is up the field, that is, near the fifty-yard line (she must never go beyond the fifty-yard line), the other fullback should be back toward the goal. The players on the defense should never be bunched in front of the goal, and in hitting the ball away from the goal, they should hit out toward the side lines—never across the center. In a corner or a bully the fullbacks should guard the goal closely.

Goal Keeper.

The goal keeper should be very cool—not get rattled if a goal is made by the opposing side. It is well for the goal keeper to watch the eyes of the opposing forward; often in that way she can tell where the forward is going to shoot. The goal keeper should never be drawn away from her goal line. She should stand about a foot in front, but no farther away. *Above all, the goal keeper should have courage; she should not step back from any ball, afraid to stop it.*

Not only should she rely on her stick, but she should remember that she may kick and stop the ball with her body. The main object is to keep the ball out of the goal and get it in less dangerous territory. This often requires quick, clear thinking on the part of the goal keeper. The fullbacks should never leave the goal keeper alone and unprotected; nor should they stand so close to her, nor so directly in front of her, that they impede her playing or obstruct her view of the play. *The goal keeper must never lose sight of the ball.*

There are a few general directions that might be given for playing. Keep your own position—don't run out of your place to interfere in someone else's. Use your head—flighty playing merely ends in wildness and nothing accomplished. Save your strength—do not use it up in the first mad rushes and terrific hits. It is the consistent, steady, dependable player who wins the game.

A great deal of time is wasted in the roll-in, that is, when the ball is put in play after going over the side line. The team taking the roll-in should have signals, that is, an understanding as to the line-up. The halfback generally takes the roll-in unless the point where roll-in occurs is near the goal line being defended, then the roll-in is taken by the fullback. The ball should be sent to the person best prepared to receive it the wing if she is free or the inside or halfback; sometimes it even may be rolled back toward the fullback.

The opponents never leave any player unguarded. As soon as the roll-in is called, it should be taken quickly.

Just as quickness is an advantage in taking the roll-in so it is in the free hit. The halfback in whose territory the foul occurred should take the free hit quickly, before her teammates may be guarded. Every delay means that the opponents have an opportunity to guard more closely. In taking the free hit, be careful to hit to an unguarded player. Make the free hit count.

In the corner play the hit should be carefully taken by the halfback, or sometimes it is taken by the wing. The attackers line up around the edge of the striking circle ready to stop the ball and shoot for the goal; the defenders are behind the line ready to rush out and get the ball away from dangerous territory. The player taking the free hit should be careful that the ball goes within the circle; that it is hit hard and cleanly—never send a ball that hops; that the ball is sent to a particular player, preferably the center forward or either of the insides. It is not often advisable for a wing to stop a ball hit in from the corner hit.

To decide a championship or the winner of a hockey tournament, it is advisable to play three games, the winner of two being the winner of the series. If one team wins the first two games it is unnecessary to play the third; if there are more than two teams contesting, it is advisable to have preliminary rounds, the winners meeting the winners, etc.

THE FIELD OF PLAY

The Field.

The dimensions of the field are: maximum length, 100 yards; minimum, 85 yards; maximum breadth, 60 yards; minimum, 55 yards. The field of play is marked by boundary lines; the end are "goal lines," and the side, "side lines." Flag posts, four feet in height, one yard outside the field of play, are placed at each of the four corners and at each end of the twenty-five-yard lines.

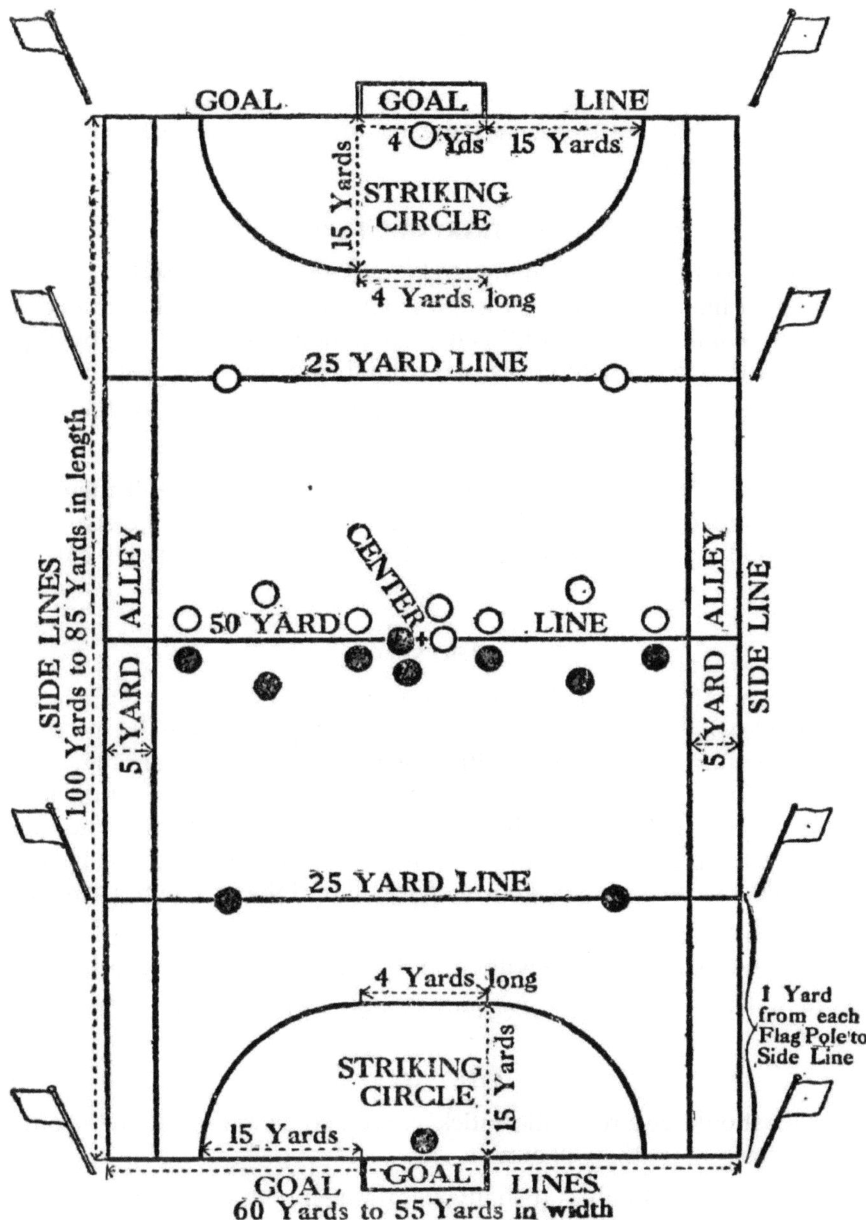

DIAGRAM OF FIELD WITH NECESSARY MARKINGS AND SHOWING THE PROPER LINE-UP OF TEAMS AT START OF GAME.

There are three lines across the field, i. e., parallel to the end lines, running from side line to side line—one in the center of field, the fifty-yard line; one at each end of the field, each twenty-five yards from the goal line.

The Goals.

The *goals* are marked by upright posts, equidistant from the corners of the goal lines, four yards apart, connected by a cross-bar seven feet from the ground. The space between the posts is known as the goal area. The maximum width of the posts and the cross-bars is two inches; the maximum depth, three inches. There is a goal at each end of the field.

The Striking Circle.

In front of each goal is a striking circle marked by the following lines: A line parallel to goal line, fifteen yards distant from, directly in front of the goal area, four yards in length. The ends of this line are joined to the goal line by a quarter circle fifteen yards in diameter measured from the nearest goal post.

A line parallel to the side line, five yards distant, is drawn the length of the field. This is called the alley.

It is important that the lines be distinctly marked in white. If there are nets behind the goal to catch balls, it aids the umpire in determining if a goal is scored. Goal posts and bar may be painted white. The ball is a leather cricket ball painted white.

Dress.

Bloomers and jumper are the most comfortable form of dress. If a skirt is worn it must be at least eight inches from the ground. Stopping the ball with the clothing is not good hockey. *Light shoes* with rubber soles, fitted for running, should be worn by the forwards and halves. Heavier shoes are worn by the fullbacks. The feet of the player ought to be well protected, in order that she may stop the ball with her feet. All players should wear *shin-guards;* the forwards and halves light ones, the fullbacks heavier. The goal keeper will find that the shin-guards used in cricket are not too heavy.

If a hat is worn, it should be without pins and must have a soft brim.

Many players prefer wearing *gloves* in order to protect their hands.

The Stick.

The *stick* should be a regulation stick, curved on one side, flat on the other. No stick must weigh more than 28 ounces.

Time.—The time of halves (usually 35 minutes) with the intermission should be determined by the captains.

Score.—Each goal made counts one point. Highest number of goals at end of game wins. There is no other score except by goals.

Officials.—There is an umpire, who makes all decisions of goals, fouls and disputes. She is responsible for the good conduct of the game. There may be an umpire for each half of the field. Also a scorer, a timekeeper and two linesmen, who call the ball out of bounds and give decisions when appealed to.

Each team has eleven players; for each side there is a *captain,* who tosses for choice of goal, protests to the umpire, governs the team on the field. They must notify the referee of any change of line-up.

FIELD HOCKEY RULES

I. Rules Governing Bully.

(*a*) The Bully is the method of putting the ball in play. A bully is played by two players, one from each team, who stand squarely opposite each other (each facing a side line), each with her right side toward her own goal. The ball is placed between them, each player having a foot on either side of the ball. Both first touch the ground on their right side of the ball, then they touch sticks. This is done alternately for three times, then either may touch the ball. After the ball is touched by either or both of the two players bullying it may be played by anyone.

(*b*) The game is started at the beginning of the first and second halves by a bully-off on the center line.

(*c*) After each goal is scored the ball is brought back to center line for bully-off, as in (*b*).

(*d*) The teams line up in a bully on the side nearest their goal line and never step over the line of the ball, i. e., an imaginary line, if ball is not on center or twenty-five-yard line drawn across field. This is known as standing behind the ball.

(*e*) After time-out is called, the ball is put in play again by bully on the spot where time-out is taken.

(*f*) If a foul is called on both teams, a bully is taken on the spot where the foul occurred.

(*g*) If any rules of bully are not observed, bully is taken over again.

(*h*) *Penalty-Bully.*—A penalty-bully can only occur when a defender inside the circle deliberately breaks a rule, thereby directly preventing a goal from being scored. The bully is played on the spot where foul occurred by goal keeper and a chosen player from the other team. All other players stand beyond the nearest twenty-five-yard line until the bully is completed. The bully is only completed when: First, a goal is scored; second, the ball is sent out of bounds by an attacker—if sent out by defender, penalty-bully is repeated; third, the ball is sent out of striking circle. In either of the first two cases the ball is put in play by a twenty-five-yard bully in the center of the nearest twenty-five-yard line. Any foul (except Rule I, *a*) by offender counts penalty goal or one point for opponents; any foul by attacker (except Rule I, *a*) the defender is given a free hit. The goal keeper in a penalty-bully may play only with the stick; she may not kick or stop ball with hands. If time is called, bully must first be completed.

II. Rules for Goal.

(*a*) To score a goal the ball must have been hit by or have touched the stick of an attacker within the striking circle.

(*b*) The ball must pass entirely over the goal line between the goal posts and under the cross-bar.

(*c*) If a ball, after touching the stick of an attacker within the circle, glances off the stick or person of a defender, it is a goal.

(*d*) If a ball hit fairly glances off a goal post across the goal line, it is a goal.

(*e*) The umpire must judge fairness of goal.

III. Rules for Sticks.

(*a*) The stick must never be raised above the shoulder in any part of the stroke while hitting the ball, nor may it be carried over shoulder. When this rule is broken within the striking circle by a defender, the penalty is a penalty-corner; if deliberately broken, it is a penalty-bully.

(*b*) The flat side, never the rounded, should be used in striking the ball.

(*c*) A player should never catch the curved part of her stick in that of her opponent's, thereby hindering her opponent's play. This is hooking.

(*d*) A player should never strike or hit her opponent's stick.

(*e*) A player should never lift her opponent's stick from the ground or in any such manner mar her stroke.

(*f*) A player should never trip an opponent with stick.

(*g*) No player without a stick may take part in play.

(*h*) For any infringement of rules, a free hit to opposing side where foul occurred is granted, unless referee deems the foul rough, thus liable to disqualification.

IV. Rules for Free Hit.

(*a*) When a team is accorded a free hit by an umpire, through a foul by opponents, the captain of the team shall designate the player (generally a halfback or fullback) who is to take the hit, and no other player may be nearer the player taking the hit than five yards. The ball must be hit squarely, not scooped. The free hit is taken again if this rule is not complied with.

(*b*) The player who has taken the free hit may not touch the ball again until it has been touched by another player.

(*c*) A foul by a defender in the striking circle upon taking a free hit is punished by a penalty-corner.

(*d*) If the player misses the ball entirely upon taking the free hit, she may hit it again.

(*e*) If there is any infringement of the rule, the free hit is given to the other side except when the ball is scooped by the defender inside the circle, when the penalty is a penalty-corner.

V. Rules for Out of Bounds.

(*a*) When the ball is sent over the side lines it shall be rolled in (by hand) by one of the team opposing the player who last touched it. In rolling in, the player taking the roll-in must stand—feet and stick—outside the side line at the point where ball went out. No player may stand inside the alley (or five-yard line) next to the side line over which it went out. The ball must be *rolled,* not thrown or bounced. It may be rolled in any direction, provided it touches within the five-yard space. The player who has taken the roll-in may not touch the ball until it has been touched by another player. The other players may step in the alley as soon as ball touches.

(*b*) First, if the ball is sent behind the goal line by an attacker; second, if a ball is unintentionally sent behind goal line by a defender more than twenty-five yards away from her goal line, it is a twenty-five-yard bully. The ball is placed on the twenty-five-yard line, exactly opposite the spot where it crossed the goal line.

(*c*) If a ball is unintentionally hit across the goal line by a defender or glances off her stick over the goal line, it is a corner. In a corner, the attackers line up around the outer edge of the striking circle—feet and sticks—behind the line, with one of their team hitting the ball to them from the corner of the field (on the side or back line not more than three yards away from the corner) on the side of the goal line where ball went out. The defenders must stand—feet and sticks—behind their goal line at least five yards away from the player taking the corner hit. The defenders may rush out as soon as the ball is hit. Before the attackers may hit the ball toward the goal, the ball must be stopped—not necessarily dead. The player taking the corner hit may not hit the ball again until touched by another. (Penalty, free hit for opposing side.) If an attacker shoots for goal before ball has been stopped, it is a free hit for opposite side. If the player taking the corner hit misses it entirely on the first stroke, she may hit it again.

(*d*) If a ball is deliberately hit over goal line by a defender, it is a penalty-corner. Both teams line up as in an ordinary corner. The hit is taken, however, from a point on the goal line at least ten yards from the nearest goal post and no opposing player may be nearer than five yards. Ball must be stopped before replayed by attacker teammate unless it has been touched by defender.

VI. Rules for Undercutting.

(*a*) The ball may not be so hit that it is lofted or raised intentionally above the shoulder.

(*b*) The ball may be "scooped" so that it may be raised moderately in air.

(*c*) Penalty for intentionally lofting is a free hit for opposing side.

VII. Rules for Offside.

(*a*) In the opponents' territory, no player may receive a ball from one of her own team standing farther from the goal than she, the receiver, unless there are at least three of her opponents between her and the goal. Violation of this rule is called offside.

(*b*) A player is not penalized for offside if she does not touch the ball; if it was touched last by an opponent; if one of her own team nearer the opponents' goal than she hits the ball; if she is in her own half of the territory.

(*c*) Penalty for offside is free hit for opposing side.

VIII. Running in on the Left.

No player shall run in on the left side of her opponent in order to gain possession of the ball so that any part of her person or stick touches any part of the person or the stick of the opponent. Penalty is free hit for opposing side.

IX. Turning on the Ball.

No player having possession of the ball shall interpose her person between the ball and an opponent, nor shall she turn around the ball in order to obtain a more favorable position for her stroke. Penalty is free hit.

X. Handling.

The ball may be caught or stopped by the hands, but must be immediately dropped perpendicularly to the ground so that no advance is made nor direction changed. It may not be picked up, carried or thrown. There shall be no shoving, pushing, or holding. If the ball stopped by goal keeper rebounds from her hand it is not a foul. Penalty is free hit.

XI. Kicking.

No player may kick the ball except the goal keeper within her own striking circle. The foot may be used to stop the ball, but must be withdrawn and not used to block opponent's stroke at the ball. Penalty is a free hit.

XII. Rough Play.

There should be no charging (rushing or running into), shinning, tripping, personal handling, impeding progress, or hitting with stick. No player may obstruct, i. e., prevent opponent from reaching the ball or prevent opponent from attacking teammate. Penalty is free hit or disqualification if umpire decides the play is rough.

XIII. Time-out.

Time-out may be called by the umpire at the request of either captain only in case of injury or accident to clothing or stick. Time-out should be called by umpire in case of loss of ball or dispute in regard to decision.

Field Hockey—1, A scrimmage for possession of the ball. 2, Getting the ball out of scrimmage. 3, Passing the ball to a teammate and away from an opponent. 4, A goal! 5, A shot. The attack has "run" the ball down the field to the striking circle—once inside the shot will be gotten off.

Basket Ball—1, The referee tosses the ball up between the opposing centers to put it in play. 2, A free trial for goal. A foul has been made and the penalized team must stand and see their opponents try for a single point.

XIV. Umpire.

The umpire, or umpires, have control of the game, and are responsible for it. They must see that there is no rough play, and that the game is played according to rules. The umpires judge goals, roll-ins, bullies, corners. They also have the power to punish players for intentionally delaying the game. The ball is in play until umpire's whistle blows.

BASKET BALL

The game; matches.

Basket ball needs no introduction. It is probably the most popular game played by girls. Through the work of the Executive Committee on Basket Ball Rules, headed by Mrs. Senda Berenson Abbott, chairman, the playing rules and the conditions under which the game may best be played have been thoroughly studied and set forth in the Spalding Official Basket Ball Guide for Women, No. 7A.

The game may be played either outdoors or indoors, depending upon conditions. When the circumstances permit it is always desirable to play out of doors. The writer is a firm believer in outdoor exercise wherever and whenever possible, but there is a decided need for a wholesome, interesting game for indoors during the long winter months. Basket ball undoubtedly fills this need.

The game is played by two teams consisting of either five, six, seven, or nine players each. If the teams play with five on a side, there are two forwards, a center and two guards each; if with six on a side, there are two centers each; if with seven, three centers; if with nine, three forwards, three centers and three guards.

The court (floor or field) is divided into three equal parts. The lines dividing the court are parallel to the end lines. They are known as field lines. The reason the court is thus divided is to define the space in which the various players may operate. Thus each set of players can operate only on their third of the court, so that the line game makes a minimum physical demand upon the player. That is, the forwards of Team A and the guards of Team B may run only in the third of the floor before the former's basket; the centers of both teams in the space in middle, and the guards of Team A and the forwards of Team B in the third of the floor before the latter's basket.

The three general positions call for three different kinds of skill. The forwards should possess a good eye, should have the knack of handling the ball well and should have agility and speed. The center should have height, ability to get possession of the ball and the knack of feeding well, that is, passing the ball to her forwards. The center rarely shoots for the basket in the line game. The guards, as their name implies, must prevent the opposing forwards from shooting a goal, so must be quick, active and able to jump well.

The game begins with each team in position. The referee puts the ball in play by tossing it up between the centers, who jump and bat it (they must not catch it). When once in play the ball must be passed from one player to another—not handled, nor rolled, nor kicked. Nor may any player carry it, but she may bounce it once, taking not more than two steps during the bounce. Thus the game is essentially one of team play, which calls for fast, clever, clean co-operation in playing. The play continues until a score is made, or a player fouls, or the ball goes out of bounds. A score is made when a player shoots the ball into the basket from the field, which counts two points for the score of her team. A foul is made when a player of one side transgresses a rule of the game—running with the ball, holding the ball more than three seconds, touching over the line with some part of person, guarding too closely, etc. When a player fouls, a free throw from a mark fifteen feet from and directly in front of the basket is allowed to a forward of the opposing side. When the ball passes through the basket, rim and net, one point is added to the score of the team.

When the ball goes over the boundary lines, the game is stopped and the ball is given to the nearest opponent of the girl who touched it last. She then passes the ball to one of her teammates, thus starting play again.

The winning of the game is determined by the scoring of the most points (both field goals and free throws) in a given time—usually fifteen-minute halves with a ten-minute intermission. Baskets are exchanged at the end of the first half.

From my own experience and observation I find the average player is weak in passing. One of the faults is inaccuracy. Every pass should count; but if the pass is wild, thrown *at* a teammate rather than *to* one, much strength and time is wasted. Throw directly to an unguarded player, or if she signals to send the pass to a certain spot, send the pass there. Think carefully what results come from a careless, inaccurate pass. It may end in fumbling, or the ball out of bounds, or the ball obtained by opponent, waste of time, delaying the game.

The passing is apt to be slow. Get the ball out of your hands as quickly as possible. To do this, every player must know the relative positions of all her teammates. She must decide the moment the ball touches her hands to whom she is going to pass, then pass quickly and carefully. By quickly I do not mean hurriedly; I mean the player should not hold the ball an undue length of time deciding what to do with it.

Many players have but one way of throwing the ball, always using the same pass. Vary your passing according to the need. If a high ball with a drop to it can be used, use it when your teammate is in a good position to receive. But do not use this style of pass exclusively. Try a short, swift pass. If when you are guarded for one pass, quickly change to another, such as, from an overhead pass—both arms holding ball high over head—to a low side pass—the arm held out toward the side, the palm of hand around the ball, which rests on the flexed hand and wrist. It takes a great deal of practice and team work to make the passing perfect, but remember always be wide awake and alert, ready to receive the ball.

Needless to say, the team work is the main factor. It is the way the team plays, not the way one player stars, that counts.

Each of the different players has a different duty to perform. The forwards have to shoot both field and foul goals. In shooting baskets, it is of prime importance to have some chosen point on basket or back board to aim at. Of course, there are many forwards who shoot at random; goals are made, but many more are missed. Once this spot for the aim is made definite—through much practice—the aim becomes surer.

Many a game has been lost through the inability to shoot foul goals. The feet should toe the 15-foot line, slightly apart, fixed firmly on the ground. The ball is held in both hands, palms flat on opposite sides of the ball; the lace is turned toward the basket. The knees are bent; the ball is carried forward and down, arms straight. Simultaneously the knees are straightened, the arms are carried forward and up, the ball leaves the hands. Just as the ball leaves the hands an "English" is put on it. That is, the ball is twirled as it leaves the hands. The advantage of the "English" lies in the fact that it serves to make the ball shoot through the basket instead of bounding out, as is often the case when it is tossed up a little off the true and without the spin.

Good passing is necessary for the forwards. The forward should remember never to shoot unless she is in a favorable position; one forward should always stick close to the basket. Always try to keep free; pass to your opponent whenever possible; never keep the ball selfishly in order to gain a shot for yourself.

The center should realize the importance of this position. Naturally the forwards cannot score goals unless the ball is sent to them. Thus, the center should be alert and quick, free to receive the pass from the guards and quick to send a good pass to her forwards, who should be dodging their guards, trying to get in a favorable position. Often the center can well make use of the bounce and step to get away from the opposing center.

The guard has to remember that every time the forward gets the ball, if she is good, she has a chance to get it in the basket. Thus, it should be the main object of the guard to get the ball away from her end of the field. Every guard should try to get the ball and send it out of dangerous territory. Then she should stick closely to her forward, guarding her as closely as the rules allow.

One fault of the guards is over-guarding. This is generally done through over-anxiety. The guards should watch carefully so as not to foul.

Jumper or middy blouse, bloomers and rubber-soled shoes make up the accepted costume.

Above all, the element of good sportsmanship and fair play should enter into every game, no matter how strenuous the playing, and the slogan of the whole team should be, "Put the ball in the basket."

Basket Ball Games or Tournament.

An umpire who is competent and fair should have entire jurisdiction over the game. The game should be conducted in an orderly fashion, according to the rules.

For a series or tournament, a set number of games should be played, such as two out of three; the winner is then the champion. If more than two teams play, the winners should play the winners, etc. Let me impress the importance of set rules agreed to and known thoroughly by every player; this saves much dispute and sometimes bitter feeling.

Leagues of basket ball teams, such as are to be found in some cities, etc., organized for the purpose of clean sport and good fellowship, have been extremely successful. Each team may play a set number of games with every other team, the winner of the most games being the champion of the league.

GYMNASTICS

Floor work; apparatus work; meet or exhibition.

Gymnastics, or work in a gymnasium, indoors or out, is recognized the world over for its utility. The term gymnastics usually applies to a group or class drilled by an instructor or coach. Gymnastic exercises may be, however, adapted to fit an individual, prescribed for her by a competent authority (which may be herself).

The very great and growing popularity of gymnastic exercise is due to several facts. First of all, there is a general awakening to the need for organized exercise at most schools and colleges and within the ranks of many social organizations. Aside from walking, gymnastic exercises, as they have been developed by the Swedes and the Germans, are possibly the most obvious form of beneficial physical exercise. Then this form of physical training has the very decided advantage of being susceptible to the widest kind of application. It may be graded so as to be beneficial to various groups of individuals of varying physical development. It may be given in the most scientific quantities—more so than any other form of exercise save walking. It may be used as a drilling force to instill discipline—against fire, for instance—in great groups of persons, for ability and sufficient knowledge in handling one's body quickly and efficiently in a crowd under abnormal conditions is quite an important and necessary accomplishment. In fact, everyone, no matter at what age, could do well by her or his body to indulge in some form of calisthenics or gymnastic exercise.

There are two main divisions of gymnastics—floor work and apparatus work.

The floor work consists mainly of tactics, calisthenics, drills with hand apparatus, such as wands, dumb bells, Indian clubs, etc., dancing and posturing exercises.

The tactics consist mainly of marching by ones, twos, threes, fours, etc., of flank marching, and of circle marching. Form in this counts for a great deal together with quick execution of commands and memory of the proper method by which the figure is to be executed. Perfect form in marching consists of the head erect, the eyes straight ahead, the shoulders back, the arms down straight at the sides, the palms of the hands turned toward the body, the fingers close together; the toes should be pointed and reach for the floor, so that the muscles of the leg and the thigh can feel the effort made. Also the marchers should observe carefully the space between each one and the straightness or regularity of the line. Watch the person ahead of you and beside you. This keeps the marching from being ragged.

In the calisthenics and drills—Indian clubs excepted—the most used exercises are: the arm stretching or raising upward, downward, sideward, forward; the bending of the head, trunk, arms, or legs; the bending of the knees; the stretching of the legs; the lunges sideward and forward; the raising and sinking on the toes. These are the fundamental exercises and may be combined to form the different drills. To attain perfect form in these, it is best to watch a competent gymnast; after so doing it is possible, by careful imitation, to attain good form yourself. These exercises may easily be practised in any sufficient space, in front of a mirror when possible. It is well to remember that form and grace are very important factors. Always keep in mind that the lines of the body should be kept symmetrical; that a lot of snap in executing the exercises is a help.

The Indian club drills consist of full arm swings, circles, dips, etc. These can best be taught by a teacher. Form is the all-important factor here also.

Dancing is divided into three separate groups: æsthetic, social, and folk dancing. The æsthetic develops the natural grace of the body; social dancing does this, too, but not to such a great extent. There are many girls who feel ungainly and unnatural in the æsthetic and social dances. For these are the folk dances. These dances are a natural expression of joy and good humor. The girl who is most unsuited to other types of dancing may enjoy and ultimately become very efficient in folk dancing.

Posturing may be added here. This is practising and attaining the correct poise and positions of the body.

Apparatus work consists of exercises on the following: stall bar, horizontal bar, parallel bar, trapeze, swinging rings, traveling rings, ropes, rope ladder, horizontal ladder, side horse, buck, etc.

The secret of success in apparatus work lies in the knowledge of muscular control and of the balance of the body. By muscular control, I mean the power to exert the proper amount of strength at the exact moment; by balance, I mean adapting the weight of the body to the strength. Apparatus work should be undertaken carefully—if possible, under the supervision of an instructor; mats should always be placed to break any fall. Too continued exercises tire even the best gymnast; sometimes the girl does not realize she is tired. Between exercises give yourself plenty of rest and relax your muscles.

As the subject is so extensive and so varied I can only mention a few exercises. The most popular pieces of apparatus seem to be the side horse, the parallel bars, and the swinging rings.

The Side Horse.—The most elementary exercises on the horse are the rests. The girl grasps the pommels of the horse and jumps to a straight-arm position; the body is straight, weight on the arms. Or she may jump to a kneeling position between the pommels; or she may jump to her toes. There are different ways of ending these exercises, either jumping back to the first position or jumping to the other side of horse. Another exercise is to run, grasp the pommels with both hands, arms straight, draw the legs up and shoot them between the pommels, landing on opposite side of the horse. The landing may be straight or by retaining a grip with one hand on the pommel, you can turn either to the left or the right, according to the hand on pommel.

Next comes the vaults. In vaulting you must remember always to jump from both feet from the center of the springboard. The best form in vaulting is gotten by keeping the arms as straight as possible; the body should be straight with toes pointing and together, the legs thrown high in the air. The different kinds of vaults which may be taken on either side are: The front vault; the face and front of the body are turned above the top of the horse, the landing is made facing the side. The flank or side vault; the side of the body is above the horse, the landing is made between the pommels with the back toward the horse. The back vault; the back of body is over the horse, the landing is the same as the side vault. The wolf vault; for the right side, the left leg passes through pommels, the right leg passes over the right pommel; as the right leg passes over the pommel, the right hand is taken away so that leg may pass; the hold is kept by the left hand. Same for left side, except leg and hand used are the left instead of the right.

Besides the vaults there are cuts, circles, dives, and inversions, which may be acquired by practice.

Parallel Bars.—As on the horse, the most elementary are the rest positions. Jumps to straight arm position at sides or ends accompanied by lifting of arms and legs, etc. It is important that every gymnast know how to swing and vault well on the bars. For the swing, the hands grasp the bars directly opposite each other. You then jump to a straight-arm position. To start to swing, the heels are drawn back, the legs brought forward and upward with free movement from the hips. The head should be held up, trunk kept erect, legs straight, toes pointed and together. For the front vault, the front of body faces the bar; for the back vault, the back of the body is over the bar.

On both the horse and the parallel bars are a multitude of cuts and circles combined with each other and with vaults.

Flying Rings.—The proper way to swing on the rings is to have the rings at such a height so that the arms are straight and the feet touch the ground comfortably. Then step backward, grasping the rings, one in each hand, until the tips of the toes just touch the ground; run forward, swing the legs forward and upward from the hips. As the body swings backward, touch the floor with both feet as if stepping; do the same on the forward swing. The legs in swinging should be kept straight both forward and backward, toes together. Another popular exercise on the rings is the inversion, that is, hanging head down, feet in air, the body straight.

There are many exercises on these three pieces of apparatus together with those on the other apparatus, for which there is not room in this book.

Gymnastic Meet or Exhibition.

An interesting event at many gymnasiums is a meet or exhibition—in case of school, college, or club, generally the results of the year's work. If these events are competitive or non-competitive, it is, for the most part, the most carefully practised work by the most proficient girls.

If these events are judged, the judges, as a rule, have a certain mark, such as 10, for each event. If the performance of the event is perfect, then the number won for that event is 10; if nearly perfect, then 9 is given, etc. The judges consider entrance; general appearance, such as neatness, regularity of order, etc.; manner of executing the exercise, such as form, position, memory, rhythm, etc.; the finish or exit. All of these factors are taken into account by the judges in scoring.

Whether for individual or group prizes, it is advisable to have competent judges who have a decided system of marking. Usually there are three judges, each marking the score independently of the others. Comparisons are made at the end of each event. The scores of all judges for each performer are added together and divided by three (or as many times as there are judges) and the result is the score for the performer.

TRACK ATHLETICS

Requirements and Explanations—Track; distances to be run; distances and arrangement of hurdles; list of junior and senior track events; jumping pits; circle for putting the shot.

Events—Sprinting; the start; hurdling; running broad jump; standing broad jump; running hop, step and jump; running high jump; standing high jump; pole vault; shot put; basket ball throw; base ball throw; hurl ball throw; javelin throw; discus throw.

Everybody knows that a certain amount of exercise is beneficial to all persons physically able to indulge. But there are still many protests against more active competitive exercise. In particular, track and field athletics for girls and women have been criticised. Of course, it is only reasonable to admit that for a girl physically unfit, over-indulgence in track work is a mistake. But in these days when the majority of schools and colleges have competent teachers for their athletic work, and when the girls are allowed to participate in events only after a thorough medical examination, the danger from track work seems to be rapidly diminishing.

Tennis, basket ball and battle ball were the first competitive sports to be widely participated in by the colleges. Miss Harriet Ballintine, Director of Physical Culture at Vassar College, thus tells of the beginning of track and field sports for women in her book, "The History of Physical Training at Vassar College": "Following basket and battle ball a demand was made for other out-of-door activities. The students became interested in hurdling, running and jumping, etc. They organized an athletic association and in November, 1895, the first field day was held. This was the beginning of track and field sports for women. Before this time there was no record of girls taking part in such competitive events. In 1896 at the Harvard Summer School a course in athletic training was opened to women. This first class was composed principally of teachers from schools and colleges whose students had asked for instruction in athletics. After Vassar's first field day many schools and colleges became interested in such contests. Previous to 1896 a course in athletics had been offered to women at the Chautauqua Summer School, but as there was no demand for it, the Harvard Summer School was, therefore, the first school to give systematic instruction to girls in track and field sports. This first class in athletics for women was in charge of Mr. James Lathrop, for many years athletic trainer at Harvard and instructor in the Theory and Practice of Athletics at the Summer School. He ordered for Miss Eva G. May, then an instructor in the gymnasium at Vassar, the first pair of spiked running shoes ever made for a woman. The Vassar

College Athletic Association provided these running shoes for every student who entered field day."

One of the main difficulties in track work at the present time is that there is no set standard for coaches and participants to use. A very creditable attempt has been made by Dr. Harry E. Stewart, Physical Director of the New Haven Normal School of Gymnastics, to collect the records made by girls and women. (See Spalding's Athletic Almanac, published annually.) However, it is not the exceptional girl who is of the record-breaking ability that should be considered entirely. Track work should be first regarded from the point of view of exercise. The equipment for track work should be supervised carefully. The clothing worn should be the lightest and the least harmful to the limbs. Light shirt waist or middy blouse, bloomers, spiked or rubber-soled shoes should be adopted. The track itself should be level and smooth, the jumping pits soft so that there is no jar, and the throwing events should have plenty of room.

One of the hardest faults to overcome in shot putting is to stay within the circle. The girl in the picture does not get all of the ground in the circle that she might, nor is her left hand helping her get the shot "up" with her right.

Track.

The track, if possible, should be a straight 100 yards. If the work is done inside it is necessary to work on the circular track or on the floor of the gymnasium. A cinder track is the most desirable if it can be procured. First the earth is dug up, then mixed with coarse ashes; the earth and coarse ashes are then packed down; fine ashes are mixed on the top layer. The whole track is then wet thoroughly and rolled until level and smooth. The track is generally divided into lanes, three feet six inches in width, and is made wide enough to have four lanes.

The last relay! The runner on the outside gives a slight advantage to her team-mate. Perhaps it is enough to counteract the advantage gained by the other team when they won the "pole."

Over the bar in the high jump. In order to successfully complete her try this jumper will have to "scissors" her left foot over.

Field Day—An exciting hurdle race.

Distances.

There are a variety of distances from 25 yards to the 100 on the straight track, and the 220 and the 440 on the circular track. A few coaches still believe that the long sprints—220 and 440—are not injurious, while others contend that the half-mile is not so harmful. However, the 50, 75, and 100-yard dashes seem to be most common at different schools and colleges. According to the records collected by Mr. Stewart, 12 seconds is the best time for the 100-yard; 8-3/5 seconds for the 75-yard; 6 seconds for the 50-yard. The other dashes noted by him are the 25-yard, 3-4/5 seconds; 30-yard, 4-3/5 seconds; 40-yard, 5-1/5 seconds; 60-yard, 8 seconds; 80-yard, 11 seconds. Also the 220-yard, 30-3/5 seconds, and 440 yard, 1 minute and 16 seconds. There is also a short relay, 300 yards, four girls, each running 75 yards. This race is very popular at the colleges.

Hurdles.

As in the running races so in the hurdles there is a wide difference of opinion as to length and as to height of hurdles and number of hurdles. The 100-yard hurdle race seems very popular, 8 hurdles, varying from 1½, 2 or 2½ feet in height. There is also the 120-yard, 10 hurdles, 14 inches high; 90-yard, 7 hurdles, 1½ and 2½ feet in height; 80-yard, 6 hurdles, 2½ feet; 65-yard, 6 hurdles, 2½ feet; 60-yard, 4 hurdles, 2½ feet; 60-yard, 3 hurdles, 2½ feet; 50-yard, 4 hurdles, 2 feet; 40-yard, 5 hurdles, 2 feet; 40-yard, 4 hurdles, 1½ feet. There is a great variety of choice.

The hurdles should be arranged: First hurdle, 15 yards from start and each hurdle 10 yards apart, allowing 15 yards between last hurdle and finish line.

In a pamphlet reprinted from the American Physical Education Review, January, 1916, "A Survey of Track Athletics for Women," Mr. Stewart has made the following selection in order to standardize track events.

Junior Events: 50-yard dash
75-yard dash
60-yard, four 2-foot hurdles
Standing broad jump
Running broad jump
Running hop, step and jump
Base ball throw
Basket ball throw

Senior Events: 50-yard dash
100-yard dash
100-yard, eight 2½-foot hurdles
Standing broad jump
Running broad jump
Running high jump
Running hop, step and jump
8-pound shot-put
Base ball throw
Basket ball throw

Mr. Stewart also says: "Only the exceptional girl should pole vault, run the 220-yard race, or put the 12-pound shot. Hurl ball (Sargent), discus (free style), javelin throw, standing high jump, and many other events are good, but the above groups seem sufficient and best adapted to competitive work."

JUMPING.

While all jumping may be done in one pit, where the space is available it is better to have one pit for the high jumps, one for the running broad, one for hop, step and jump, another for the pole vault.

The pits should be soft. All pits are made the same way but differ in size. The earth should be dug up to a depth of at least a foot and a half. If ground is hard, pits should be deeper. This soft dug-up earth should be equally mixed with sand or sawdust or both. Pits should be kept well raked up and not allowed to become packed.

For the high jump the pit should be wide, at least eight feet in width and six or seven feet long. For high jumping, two adjustable standards and a bamboo or thin cross-bar are required. These standards are placed six feet apart, directly opposite each other in a straight line. The standards are perforated by little round holes into which the pegs (not more than 3 inches long) are inserted to hold the cross-bar. There should be a runway or approach of at least twenty yards. There is *no take-off*.

For the running broad jump there is a runway—cinder track, if possible—20 to 30 yards in length, 3 feet in width. A take-off is sunk, marking division between runway and pit. This is a planed joist, 5 inches wide, sunk into ground so that top is on a level with runway, and painted white. The pit should be at least 25 feet long and about 6 feet wide. This may also be used for standing broad. The pit for the hop, step and jump is constructed in the same way.

For the pole vault the uprights should be 10 feet apart, placed opposite each other. There is a runway—cinder track, if possible—about 20 or 25 yards long, 10 feet wide. Between the two uprights a plank 16 inches deep should be sunk, 2 inches of which should be above ground level. In front of plank, in center, a hole 5 or 6 inches deep should be dug.

Putting the Shot.

The contestant stands in a 7-foot circle and the put or throw must be made from within the circle. It is a foul for either foot to touch the ground outside until the shot has landed. A toe board raised 4 or 5 inches above the ground and sunk firmly into the earth should form about one-quarter of the circle. Spalding's official 8 and 12-pound shots are used.

Sprinting.

From my own observation, I have seen few girls that really know how to run. One great trouble is that the instinct is to run as speedily as possible from the minute you get on the track. First of all you should learn to run well in good form. I shall try to give a few hints to the runner which may be helpful.

Head.—The head should be up, the eyes looking straight ahead and firmly fixed on the finish line.

Shoulders.—The shoulders should be kept straight up and back, not allowed to wiggle from side to side.

Body.—The whole trunk from waistline up, however, should be bent slightly forward.

Arms.—The arms should be held loosely in a bent position, the forearm at right angles with the upper arm. The movement of the arms should be controlled; they should be allowed to swing forward and backward in accordance with the motion of the rest of the body. Many runners do not control the swinging of the arms, letting them flap sideward, downward, thus wasting energy. Some runners use cork grips for the hands; personally, I prefer to run with my hands clenched into a fist.

Legs.—Many runners make the mistake in thinking the longer your stride, the better your form and the faster you run. If you have a long stride it is often apt to be very helpful, but the runner should not try to take an abnormally long stride. By that I mean take only as long a stride as you can manage without strain, or without appearing to be running in leaps and bounds. Neither should the knees be dashed high in front.

Feet.—A great deal in running depends upon the way the feet are placed. The toe of the foot should reach out for the ground; the toe should be pointed straight ahead and each foot should be put down on the ground directly in front of its former position. The runner should take care not to run heavily, and she should, whether in practice or competition, always stride well up on her toes.

In running you should always think of yourself as a unit, running with the smoothest possible action. Some runners are not units, but arms, legs, body and knees, all wobbling in different ways, giving the general appearance of falling apart. Yet you must not go too far the other way, that is, don't run tensely. Be limber but not loose. Try to get all the spring and lightness possible. To do this get the balance over the feet; don't run with balance too far forward or too far back.

The Start.—The crouch start is conceded to be the best. This should be practised until the runner learns to get away at the word "go," to get the proper push with the rear leg, and to rise to an upright position gradually. There are three counts for the crouching start: "Get ready." The fingers are placed just behind starting line; the arms should be carried straight down from the shoulders, thus making the hands shoulder width apart; the runners then kneel on one knee, either right or left, according to preference; the toe of the forward foot should be as close to starting line as is comfortable for runner; the knee of rear leg should be on a line with front leg, close up to it, with lower part of leg (that is, below the knee) reaching back as far as possible in a straight line from the knee. A hole should be dug for the toe of each foot. "Get set." The rear knee is raised, the whole body tense ready for the spring; the weight is thrown over the front knee so that the toe of front foot feels the weight and can get a good push over; the head is up; the whole strength of the body seems concentrated in the muscles used in springing forward. "Go" (or the pistol shot). The sprinter springs forward with all the force possible from the front foot. But she should not assume an upright position at once, but gradually, after three or four strides have been taken. In other starts you stand upright with one leg back, other leg front. Front leg is slightly bent, weight of body is over front leg.

HURDLING.

In hurdling, the crouching start is very important. All the form of sprinting should be considered and also there should be perfect form over the hurdles. A girl may be a fast runner, but if she cannot take the hurdles well and quickly she will be defeated by a slower girl who can. Many hurdlers twist toward the side, or, in landing, land too far to one side of hurdle. First the approach from the start to the first hurdle should be carefully measured by strides. The runner should always take just this number of strides. The strides between each hurdle should be counted also. Then a mark should be made in front of each hurdle, from which point the hurdler should always rise to the hurdles. The long low stride is the best over the hurdles. There are two forms of hurdling, that of the leg bent sideways, usually recommended for girls, and the "straight-leg." For the first, the front leg—leg first over the hurdle in the stride—is bent across the other leg; the arms are stretched out toward the side; the rear leg is trailed over the hurdle; the front foot reaches the ground first, the hurdler landing squarely on the ball of the foot, the toe pointed straight ahead. Personally, I prefer the "straight-leg" hurdle to the "side-leg" style. In the latter the rise over the hurdle is greater, the upright position of the trunk meets more resistance from the air, the landing is made with more of a jar. In the "straight-leg" the stride over hurdle is long and as low as possible; the body is bent as far over the front leg as possible; the front leg shoots over the hurdle straight, for as great a distance as possible, the arm (on same side of body) is forward when leg is; the rear leg is trailed, extending slightly to the side from the thigh to the toe; the weight of body is as far forward as possible, thus enabling a longer stride; the front foot should land on ground, on the ball, toe pointed forward; the rear foot should be ready to shoot out for next stride. My advice is for hurdlers to practice until they are sure of themselves before running in a race. They must not hesitate before hurdles, thus forced to jump off both feet. The rise should be with the least possible effort; the landing should be light, the runner immediately resuming the stride. Never be afraid of a hurdle. Practice until you are perfect and sure of yourself, and sure of the hurdle. Confidence makes you successful.

Running Broad Jump.

There are two important parts to the running broad jump—the run and the jump. The run should not be so long as to tire the jumper. The first few strides are slow, then at a mark placed by the jumper the speed increases until the take-off is reached. The momentum gathered in this run aids in the jump greatly, thus it is important that a mark be made the proper number of strides away from the take-off. The foot which takes the jump from the take-off should always be the same one, therefore the strides before the take-off should be carefully observed.

A spring is made when the foot lands on the take-off. It is a foul to step over the take-off. After the jumper has given the best leap possible from the ball of the foot on the take-off, she tries to augment this leap by drawing her legs up under her, throwing her arms up and forward. When nearing ground the feet should shoot forward, the whole body thrown so that the balance is forward. This insures a better landing. The jump should be high. Many coaches teach the girls to jump over a bar, thus forming a habit of getting height. It is always well to fix your eye on a point about four feet high and beyond the distance you can jump. Fix your eye on this at the beginning of the run and keep it there until a landing is made.

Standing Broad Jump.

The jumper stands with both feet on the take-off, toes overlapping the outer edge to get a grip. Many jumpers like to rock back and forth on the toes, knees slightly bent; the arms also are swung gently backward and forward. When the jumper is ready to spring, the arms should be held above the head and brought back with a snap as the spring is made, with the knees bent forward and all the strength concentrated for the jump. As in the running broad, the jump should be high, thus the eyes should be fixed on a spot high and beyond the distance you expect to jump. While in the air, shoot the arms, legs and body as far forward as possible in order to gain distance.

Running Hop, Step and Jump.

The run is the same as in the running broad jump, except at the end instead of jumping you first take a hop, immediately followed by a step and then a jump. The hop ends on the same foot which landed on the take-off; then the step, the opposite foot landing on the ground; then the jump is taken from the foot then on the ground. The greatest effort should be in the jump; the other two should not take such a lot of effort that the speed is slowed up.

Running High Jump.

As in the running broad jump, the girl should have a mark by which she can tell the point where her speed should be increased. The same foot should always be brought to the same position for jumping; thus, the number of strides should be carefully taken from the mark to the bar every time. Some jumpers approach from the left, some from the right. The spring is taken from the ball of the foot nearest to the bar at a distance determined by practice, usually three to four feet. The nearer leg is thrown over the bar. As the nearer leg is thrown high, the far leg with a strong push leaves the ground; thus, as the near leg is coming down the far leg is going up and over the bar. It is often advisable to throw the body away from the bar.

It is bad form to touch or knock the cross-bar.

Standing High Jump.

The form of the standing high is the same, except that the jumper stands about a foot away from the bar, side turned toward it. As in the broad jump, she may gather speed by swinging the arms and rocking on the toes until strength is summoned for the spring. The feet must not leave the ground until the spring is made.

Pole Vault.

As in the jumps, the pole vaulter must determine her run to the point where the foot makes the spring. She should run slowly until the point for the faster run is marked, then she should gather speed and come to the spot from which spring is taken. The spring should always be taken from the same foot, and the run should always start with this foot.

The pole should be grasped with both hands, the palm of the lower hand facing inward and the top hand outward. The vaulter should grasp the pole at the height of the cross-bar, which she measures on pole at each increase of height and at each trial.

During the run the pole is held across the body, with the hands gripping the pole at proper spot; then the pole is placed in the hole in front of cross-bar and a spring is taken from the foot; the arm underneath should be straight, the one above bent; as the pole swings to a vertical position the body swings up, and if the vaulter is strong enough in the arms she should slide the lower hand up to the top one; an extra push is given to propel the body over the bar as the pole is released. While crossing the bar the body should be arched; in falling, the face should be downward. The landing should be easy and light.

Shot Put.

The competitor must stay within the circle and must not step over the toe board. If the shot is held in the right hand, the left side of the body is turned in the direction shot is going; the weight is on the right foot, the left foot and left arm are raised to help the balance of the body; the shot is carried in right hand, which is held up slightly above the shoulder, elbow of right arm bent and well back, and held as close as possible to the ribs. A quick hop forward is taken, the same position is retained; then the body is turned, the weight transferred to the left leg, and as this is done the shot is thrust forward, with the weight and entire strength of body behind the throw; the right foot comes forward to preserve the balance; the toe should be against the springboard.

It is important to learn the correct form in shot putting, thus it is advisable to practice with a light weight.

Basket Ball Throw.

This throw is similar to the shot put in form, the ball being held high over the body. It is a foul to step outside the circle, 6 feet in diameter. The ball also may be thrown from the flexed wrist position, that is, the ball rests in palm of hand and on the bent wrist. In both the throws the ball is thrown after a spring on the right foot is taken. It is better to throw the ball high.

Base Ball Throw.

As in the basket ball throw, the base ball throw should have height. The throw must be an overhand throw and the competitor must not step out of the circle. The ball is grasped by some people by the first two fingers and the thumb, the other two fingers are bent into the palm.

Hurl Ball Throw.

The regulation hurl ball has a short strap on it. This strap is grasped in one hand; the side of body is turned in direction the ball is going; the ball is carried high overhead and then down, describing a circle; a hop forward is taken, the ball released as it is starting up—this then insures height.

Javelin Throw.

The javelin is grasped by one hand or by both hands. The center of balance is found on the javelin; here it is gripped by the hand, the first and second fingers and thumb holding it; the hand should be over the shoulder; a short run should be taken; then, with right foot back and all the weight on it, the javelin is carried back; then the arm, shoulder, and body come quickly forward, the hand releases the javelin and the weight is on the left (forward) foot. The competitor may not cross the board or the mark.

Discus Throw.

The discus is thrown in two ways:

1. Free Style.—The discus is held in the palm of the right hand, the edge resting between the first and second joints of the fingers. The flight is guided by means of the index finger. The right hand is swung down and across the body; the right foot is at the rear of circle, the left a little forward; when the right hand has been swung back to the maximum reach of the arm, the thrower should pivot on the left heel, then she should crouch, straighten body and throw the discus, making a spring so that the feet are changed; thus, right foot is back, left forward.

2. Greek Style.—This is generally from a block or pedestal; the competitor, right leg forward, holds the discus in both hands overhead, then the discus is shifted to the right hand, which is brought down and back as far as possible. The knees are bent. Now the knees are straightened, a jump forward is taken and discus is hurled in the air.

* * * * *

The main difficulty with track athletics is that they are overdone, that is, a girl does not consider her strength. In training a horse, the trainer does not urge it to tear over the course two or three times at full speed. This is just the way some girls think they are improving their running or jumping, getting to the top form sometimes two or three times a day.

It is advisable to practice for form slowly at first, then increase your effort. In this way then your maximum effort can be made when you are perfect in form and condition; not too jaded by overwork to do your best or so used to hurried efforts that your form is neglected.

One of the great troubles with girls in athletics is that they pitch in too strenuously, with too much enthusiasm. This exuberance should be carefully diverted into the proper channels by the coach. Confine yourself to a few events, all of which you can do well. It is a useless waste of energy to spend your strength in events for which you are too tired to perfect your form. Not only do you owe to your coach and your school or college the responsibility for your good health, but to yourself. Therefore never over-exert in track work.

A coach plays a very great part in track athletics and should watch closely over the girls. If any of them seem tired or stale, let them rest for three or four days. Don't, in your desire and enthusiasm, forget that more harm may be done through overwork and too strict training than in more obvious ways.

HOW TO CONDUCT A TRACK MEET

The Competitors.

Every athlete should be entered in the meet a sufficient time before in order that the places, events and handicaps may be arranged. Handicaps may be granted if a mediocre runner is running with one of stellar ability. Every athlete should have a number.

The Officials.

Referee.—The referee has entire charge of the meet and is responsible for the good conduct of the meet. All fouls are dealt with by her. She may disqualify an offender and give the runner fouled another trial, or allow a new race to be run.

The Clerk of the Course.—This position deals mainly with the executive part of the meet. The clerk of the course sees that the events are run in order and on scheduled time. She sees that the contestants are called on time for their events. She also assigns the contestants to their places—1st, 2nd, 3rd lane, etc.—for the races.

Starter.—The starter gives the signal. As a rule, the pistol is the signal for the start. The starter should have a blank cartridge pistol, which she fires up into the air. The signals are: (1) "On your mark!" (2) "Get set!" (3) "Pistol." The starter may penalize for a false start or for beating the pistol, that is, anticipating the pistol shot. She may disqualify if a runner deliberately starts ahead of the mark.

Inspectors.—These officials watch for fouls in a race, such as, impeding a runner; coaching during the race; crossing into another lane; grasping tape in hands; knocking over a hurdle.

Judges at Finish.—These judge the order of the runners at finish line—1st, 2nd, 3rd, etc.

Timekeeper.—The timekeeper must use a stopwatch and must stand at the finish line. As soon as a runner touches tape or crosses line the timekeeper stops her watch, which was started at pistol shot. There should be at least one timekeeper for each of the first three runners.

Field Judges.—These judges have entire charge of field events.

Scorer.—Scorer keeps the official places and times of the participants.

Races.

The Start.—First false start is penalized a yard; second, a yard more; third, disqualifies. Any foul during race or start disqualifies. A tape or strand of worsted is stretched (about four feet high) across the track; the winner must breast this tape, arms raised. Every other runner must cross the finish line.

In a hurdle race the hurdles are placed 15 yards from start and 15 yards from finish line, allowing 10 yards in between each hurdle. The hurdler may knock down or over two hurdles and still win, but she is disqualified for the third. No record stands if a hurdle has been knocked over. All other rules for racing hold.

In the relay race the first girl to run starts at pistol; she or each succeeding runner must touch the hand of or hand the baton to the following runner. The last girl running must cross the finish line. No runner may run twice in a relay. All other rules for races are the same.

Jumping.—Each competitor may have three trials, but she may take but one or two of those if she prefers.

Running Broad Jump.—It is a foul to touch the ground with the foot on the farther side of the take-off. This counts as one trial. It is a foul to balk, that is, to run over the take-off without jumping. The longest jump is scored. The distance is measured by a field judge from the take-off to the nearest mark left by jumper.

Standing Broad Jump.—It is a foul to take a preliminary spring or jump or to touch the earth in front of take-off with the foot. Measurement same as running broad jump.

Running Hop, Step, and Jump.—Fouls and measurements same as running broad.

Running High Jump.—Each competitor has three trials for each height. Unless she clears the bar without knocking it off it is a failure. It is counted a trial if the runner balks and does not jump. It is counted a trial to grasp the cross-bar. The bar is fixed at different heights; it is also well to measure bar in middle to determine exact height.

Standing High Jump.—No preliminary jump or spring may be made. Measurement is the same as in running high jump.

Pole Vault.—Each has three trials for each height. A vaulter is allowed to balk—that is, run without vaulting—but two balks count as a try. If the cross-bar is knocked off it is a failure.

Weight Throwing.—Each has three trials. The distance is measured from the toe board to the nearest mark left by shot. It is a foul to touch with any part of person over the toe board or out of circle. It is a foul to throw the shot instead of putting it straight out from the shoulder. It counts as a try to drop the shot.

Base Ball Throw.—Same as shot put.

Basket Ball Throw.—Same as shot put.

Javelin Throw.—Same as shot put.

Discus Throw.—Same as shot put.

Score.—The score for first place is generally 5 points; second place, 3 points;

third, 1 point. If there is a tie the competitors divide the points. If tied for first place, the sum of first and second points is divided; same for tie for second place.

FIELD DAY

Field Day is essentially one on which field sports are participated in. It is usually held annually. By field sports are meant the throws, the weight and jumping events described in the chapter on Track Athletics. Field Day, however, has various interpretations; it may be for celebration, or for exhibitions, or for competition. As the title indicates, Field Day is an out-of-door function.

If it is a gala day for celebration, there may be different kinds of dances—interpretative dances, æsthetic dances, May pole dancing, and folk dances; there may be drills of various kinds, such as are mentioned in the chapter on Gymnastics; there may be tournament meets or games.

Field Day as an exhibition may consist of different dances, drills and sports, or games that have been practised during the year and that are displayed now in order to show the results obtained.

The Field Day in which dancing and drills play an important part is often enlivened by the use of colors. Scarfs, streamers or bands of striking colors lend an effective note to a dance. For the drills a uniform costume with a distinguishing streak of color is the most suitable. As modern people like to be entertained, mock games, "stunts," and such races as three-legged, sack, and potato, may be used. The object of the "mock games" and "stunts" is to amuse as much as possible. There is very little element of sport that enters in. In the games, players used to certain positions may play entirely different ones; or they may be dressed up in popular "take-offs" (imitations).

The third interpretation of Field Day is one for the purpose of holding competitive sports or games. In fact, Field Day is often held annually to decide the winners or the champions in the sports indulged in during the year; or Field Day is the day of the annual track and field meet. A method for competition in each sport is suggested at the end of each respective chapter.

WALKING

Tramps or hikes; competitive walking.

There is a vast amount of difference between a real walk and a so-called walk. A saunter along the city streets in high-heeled pumps and clothing too restricted to allow a free stride and room for deep breathing is not a real walk, especially as it usually consists of stops, such as gazing at shop windows or sampling the confections of the various stores. A real walk is entirely different, with the walker reaping all the benefits derivable from fresh air and muscular activity. There are two kinds of real walking—non-competitive and competitive.

To deal first with non-competitive walking, which is for the sheer joy of exercise and fresh air, there are three maxims to be remembered by the walker, namely, distance, form and clothing.

Distance.—The walker should have an objective point, but the distance should never be longer than can be accomplished without extreme effort. It never pays to over-exert. When tired, the walker should rest or stop, but never give up when the tired feeling is merely imaginary. Cover up well when resting or upon stopping. The main trouble often is that an unaccustomed walker will try to keep pace with a walker of long experience. The unaccustomed walker is then apt to walk too fast, too far or too long. Be conservative in the distance at first, then increase it as your experience increases.

Form.—Many walkers fail to derive entire benefit from their exercise because they walk badly. The head should be up, shoulders erect, chest forward, so that there is plenty of room for deep breathing. How many walkers fail to breathe deeply and gloriously! How many walkers gasp for breath and puff and plod along the way! Then the arms often are allowed to swing too violently, thus wasting a lot of energy. Watch your arms; don't let them imitate pump handles. Let them move freely but gently. The legs, of course, are kept straight; the foot should be put down so that the toe and ball of foot are on the ground a fraction of a second before the heel. Be careful that you don't come thundering down on your heels or come down with the whole foot flat.

Clothing.—The importance of clothing is often disregarded, for the most part through thoughtlessness. The shoes worn should be comfortable—low-heeled, broad toes, a medium rubber or leather sole. The skirt should be short enough and wide enough to allow perfect freedom of stride. The clothing around the body should be loose enough to allow free play of the muscles and ample chest expansion. Dress warmly, but do not start with so much clothing that you will soon become overheated.

Tramps or Hikes.

One of the most enjoyable forms of walking is a weekly series of tramps or hikes. This is an extremely beneficial form of outdoor exercise for a school or a club to indulge in. Everybody can join in. A leader should be appointed or elected and a committee chosen to arrange a schedule of tramps. Start out with an objective point of local or historical interest that will make a walk of not more than four or five miles for the first attempt. The distance can be gradually increased as the walkers become accustomed until finally they can take all day trips. Such a day spent by a jolly group of girls gives not only valuable physical development but also combines exercise with social enjoyment.

Good advice to the walker is: Breathe deeply; walk briskly; take a walk as often and as regularly as possible although it may be but a short one.

Competitive Walking.

Competitive walking may be for distance—greatest distance in a set time; or for time—fastest time for a set distance. As in all competitive sports, competitive walking should be watched for over-exertion, nerve strain and exhaustion. In the walk the arms are bent; one foot must be on the ground when other is off or the official will call a foul for running. The form is called the "heel and toe" walk, the heel of one foot leaving the ground as the toe of other foot comes down.

The rules for walking are very similar to those of running or sprinting. The competitor must start from behind a starting line, at a given signal, usually a gun. The distance of the race is measured and there is either a tape to be breasted or a finish line on the track to be crossed. False starts are penalized as in track (Page 41). Two fouls making the offender liable to disqualification are: running, i. e., having both feet off the ground at the same time; interfering with or impeding another competitor.

A hike in the open is one of the best ways for a group of girls to spend a day. These girls are not hampered by cumbersome clothes—doubtless they are all enjoying themselves and learning the wonders of nature.

Ice Hockey—Dribbling the puck down the ice, defending players have covered the teammates of the dribbler to prevent a successful pass. At the same time the defense is alert to stop the dribble.

GOLF

Golf, like tennis, is a favorite outdoor game. It is essentially an open weather game, but it may be played all the year around. It is deservedly popular because it combines cross-country walking, with all of its many benefits, and a peculiar skill with a variety of implements or clubs.

Anybody—woman, girl or child in her teens—who has perseverance can make a golfer. No great strength is necessary. The only requisites are a good eye, persistence, a good teacher and the facilities of a course. Fortunate is the person who at an early age learned his or her golf from a competent instructor, and fortunate is the person who has the facilities of a golf course either public or private.

The standard golf course is of eighteen holes. The average hole is 300 yards or more, although the distances usually vary from 125 yards to 600 yards and of a total length of upward of 6,000 yards. Should a player play straight over the course it will be seen that a single round would usually require a walk of four miles. Play is started from a driving green—a leveled mound of earth. The ball is teed-up on the driving green by placing a pinch of fine sand on the green and the ball upon it so that it is a half inch or more above the surface. The driver, a wooden club with a heavy head or sole, is used and the ball sent with a full stroke as far on its way to the hole as possible. Usually the space immediately in front of the tee for 50 or 75 yards is rough ground, terminating with a bunker and sand pit or some other form of hazard such as a brook, etc. Then comes the fair green, a more or less level grassy stretch extending to within a few yards of the putting green, which contains the hole or cup. On either side of the fair green is the rough, which is long grass, sand, water and other hazards. Usually the putting green is surrounded by traps such as sand pits, bunkers or mounds of earth and water hazards, while often a brook trickles through the fair green. The object of the game is to negotiate the course in the fewest number of strokes.

The drive from the tee should carry one over the first rough and over the first bunker or trap and well on to the fair green. On the fair green, if the hole is a long one and the lie of the ball favorable, the club used to send the ball again on its way is the brassie, which is a wooden club quite similar to the driver. It has a wooden head or sole, but the bottom of the head is plaited with a strip of brass to protect the wood, as the ball must be picked up off the ground without the aid of teeing. The drive for a girl should net a hundred yards, more or less, and the brassie stroke about the same. Often the lie of the ball on the fair green is not favorable to a brassie stroke, in which case an iron club with a pitch to the head of the club with which to loft the ball is used. This may be the mid-iron, the cleek, the mashie-niblic, or the mashie. The last named club is sometimes called the lofter and is used mainly for approaching the hole from off the green from distances of a hundred yards or less. The putting green is a very well levelled surface of extremely fine grass in which the cap is sunk. Putting greens vary from very fine levels likened to billiard tables to undulating slopes. The club to use on this green is the putter.

When a player is unfortunate enough to send the ball into the rough or long grass, a heavy iron club such as the mashie-niblic or mid-iron is used. And when the ball is sent into the sand or in a bunker the niblic is played. This club has a very heavy sole with a decided pitch for lofting and sends the ball high into the air out of trouble and on to the fair green when the stroke is played properly.

In learning to putt, the game of Clock Golf, found on most good courses, is a great help for it means that a girl may get diversion while *grasping* the fundamentals. The first question in putting, as with every club, is *to establish the most efficient grip*. There are two classes of grips—the overlapping grip and the regular or two-handed grip. The *former is the more modern grip and is, I believe, the more efficient*. The left hand is placed nearly at the end of the club. The right hand is so placed that the little finger of the right overlaps the first finger of the left, and the left thumb is almost entirely covered by the right hand. This grip brings the wrists closer together than the two-handed method and so produces greater harmony of action in the swing.

With the grip established, the next fundamental is the stance and address. Draw an imaginary line from the ball to the hole; stand behind the line with heels together—feet at right angles to each other, the left foot pointing toward the hole; the player stands bending slightly from the hips with arms stretched down full length; the right elbow points to the right thigh; the left points toward the hole; the club swings as a pendulum; the sole of the club addresses the ball at right angles to the imaginary line. The player's eye should be right above the ball. The secret of the putt is two-fold—the swing, which should be in direct proportion to the distance (and state of the green) from the hole, and the impact of club and ball at a perfect right angle. The follow through should be along the imaginary line still preserving the right angle. With the fundamentals established, practice will develop astonishingly accurate putting.

When the beginner has become adept at putting, the next step is to place the ball back on to the fairway twenty yards or so and take up the mashie. Here again the fundamentals are important. The grip is already mastered. The stance however differs in that the heels are not together—the feet being farther apart, the right foot farther behind the ball. The stance and address are important and the player should obtain the advice of a professional or seasoned player. The best advice the writer can give is to study the club and let it do its work. The mashie can be used for a chip stroke for short distance and for a full stroke when the ball lies farther from the hole. It is an extremely important club and when mastered can save the player many strokes.

The next club to study is the brassie. The stroke with the brassie is the same as with the driver on the tee. The stance and address for the drive and the brassie shot finds the player with feet well apart, the right foot well behind the ball, the arms extended, the body upright and flexible, the weight evenly on both feet and the head down with the eye somewhat behind the ball. The club addresses the ball at right angles. In the upward swing of the club the forearms are turned and the left knee shifts so as to bring the weight on to the right foot; the club descends down through the arc it has described; the right foot pivots, the forearms turn, the weight comes almost wholly on the left foot and the club returns to the ball exactly at right angles. The club head is ahead of the hands and the ball is hit cleanly, the power coming from the right arm. The follow through finds the weight on the left foot, the right having only enough to preserve the player's balance.

It is on the drive and brassie stroke that "pressing" is a severe fault. It is more important to hit true and to preserve the right angle by following through than to hit hard. Most girls do not hit a long ball. A far surer game is the short game. Accurate strokes down the middle of the fair green is sounder golf, so do not "press" and do not try to kill the ball.

After the brassie and driver are mastered, one can take up the mid-iron, cleek, niblic, spoon, and jigger in the order named. These clubs are for special service, and cannot be described in detail here.

An excellent practice to follow when taking up the game for the first time is to devote a day or even a week to each club, although it takes will-power to resist playing with the whole set instead of one club. As you master a club practice with it continuously. You will find such practice invaluable. Do not take up your second club until you have thoroughly mastered the first. And as I have said before, I would recommend that the game be learned backward—so to speak—with putter first, then with mashie, brassie, driver and down through the other clubs.

An adjacent golf course is a welcome requisite to a girls' school or club. It is desirable for athletic associations or faculties to organize tournaments, as competition usually heightens interest. Where skill is unequal handicaps may be arranged by averaging a player's scores and allowing the differences between the average score and par as a handicap. In this way evenness in competition is assured. Usually matches are decided by the winning of holes, although many competitions are decided on medal score or the total strokes for 18 holes. There are several kinds of tournaments possible in golf—two-ball or four-ball matches, or best ball matches. The last is where four players go around the course, two playing against the other two and counting only the best ball on each hole. Possibly the most satisfactory form for a tournament to take is the round robin tournament, where the number of entries is not too great, as each player meets everyone entered. Where the entry list is big the elimination tournament is most efficacious, and when there is still a larger entry list it is well to divide the players into first and second flights by first playing a qualifying round, counting medal scores, the lowest scores being grouped together in the first flight. A match may be made even by handicaps when players of varying skill are entered.

SKATING

There are few forms of exercise that are more exhilarating than skating. There seems to be a peculiar fascination that holds you. There is a pleasing restfulness and a soothing feeling while you are gliding over the smooth ice. Surely there is nothing so interesting to watch as good skating. An intangible quality seems to draw you to it, to make you want to put on a pair of skates and try it yourself. Out-of-doors skating is, of course, preferable to rink skating, but the latter is a very acceptable substitute.

"I have weak ankles. I can't skate." How many times have girls offered this trite excuse! If anyone really wants to learn to skate, with a little patience and perseverance it can soon be accomplished.

The skates should be the right size for the shoe in order to avoid any accident. The shoe should be high, and not too stiff at the ankles. It is advisable to have the shoe and skate fastened together. The skates should be always well wiped, sharp and in good condition.

The skater must learn straight skating, that is, moving forward by long slides on each foot alternately while the foot not on the ice is held up backward and outward from the ice, before attempting intricacies.

To learn the elementals of straight skating, start with the left foot. This foot slides forward on the flat of the skate, the toe turned out; the left knee is bent, the weight of the body is forward, thus giving momentum to the slide. The right foot is back, raised a few inches. When the momentum is almost gone, then gripping the ice with the toe of the left foot, the right foot starts its slide. As the right starts, the left foot is lifted ready for the glide, and so on, skating straight ahead.

Skating backward is learned in the same manner, except that the back of the foot is turned out instead of the toe.

It requires practice in order to perfect these two forms of straight skating. They should be acquired and thoroughly mastered, so that the skater glides over the ice with ease and skill before any dancing or continental skating is attempted.

There are several points of form that should be brought to mind. The slides or strokes should always be of equal length and as long as possible. If one foot is stronger than the other, then particular attention should be paid to the weaker foot. The skating knee is always bent. The foot not in use is stretched outward and downward, toe pointed downward. The body is carried well forward, head erect; the arms move rhythmically, but not in an exaggerated position. The body must not be stiff. There should be no rigid muscles at all.

It is not the hurried, quick strides with a body bent over in a grotesque fashion that constitutes good skating, but the long, even glides, with the body poised naturally and responding to the rhythm of the motion.

Continental skating has in the last few years proved to be very popular. It is impossible to give a detailed account of all the intricate figures in a comparatively limited space. The more elementary school figures, however, can easily be explained. The skate has an inside and an outside edge, and progress may be made either forward or backward on either edge. Thus, there are four edges: forward outside edge, backward outside edge, forward inside edge, backward inside edge.

For the forward outside edge a circle is described on the outer edge of the skate. The first stroke is on the right foot. The start is obtained by a push from inside edge of the skate of the left foot. The body leans toward the circle.

For the backward outside edge, the circle is described on the outer edge of the skate. This is like the forward outside edge, only much more difficult; the body leans in toward the circle and backward.

The forward inside edge is a circle described on the inside edge of the skate; the outer shoulder is turned as far out and forward, the inner shoulder is turned back, the body leans toward the middle of the circle. When the circle is almost complete, the free foot is brought forward, the shoulders straightened.

The backward inside edge is more difficult, but the theory is the same as the forward inside edge. The foot at completion is carried back, not forward, however.

These are fundamentals for figure skating and should be practised carefully. After the edges, the five threes, the loops, the brackets, the four rockers, and the four counters are learned. These are easily learned if the four edges have been perfected.

ICE HOCKEY

One of the most enjoyable and thrilling of the skating pastimes is ice hockey. For this a special hockey skate is made.

How the Game is Played.

The game is played by two teams with six or seven players. The players hit a small piece of rubber, called the puck, with sticks especially made. These sticks are long and slender, flat at the blade, which is at an angle from the handle. The ball is advanced up and down the rink or playing area. A point is scored when one team shoots the puck through the opponents' goal. The team wins which has the highest number of points at the end of the game, which is divided into two halves of twenty minutes each with a ten-minute intermission between the halves.

The playing area is usually 112 feet long by 58 feet wide. There are two goal posts at each end of the playing area, 10 feet from the edge of the ice; the posts are 4 feet high and are 6 feet apart. A sloping net should be placed in back to catch the balls.

The game is started with the puck in the middle of the ice, i. e., the referee places the puck between the sticks of two opposing players, each of whom tries to get possession of the ball or pass it to one of her teammates. The game is a very fast one. The four forward players, the rover (right center) and the left center, and the right and left wings, are essentially attackers, although the rover may be called upon to defend. Cover point, point, and goal keeper are the defense players. The goal keeper should stick close to her goal; the point plays in front of the goal, some distance from her; the cover point plays some distance in front of the point and can often aid the forwards by feeding them and assuming an aggressive play.

If the puck goes out of bounds over the end lines it is faced, by the referee, five yards within the goal line and at right angles to it. If it goes over the side lines it is faced five yards within the line and at right angles to it.

The puck is played by means of the stick. It is not permissible to touch it with any part of the body, except to stop it dead or block it. The puck may be pushed, shoved, or lifted, i. e., by inserting the blade of the stick under the puck. You may hit your opponent's stick.

You may body check, that is, shove from the side or front with the shoulder or hip.

You may block an opponent or you may block the puck with the skates, stick, or body.

An important rule is that of off-side. No player, if she is between the puck and her opponent's goal, may receive a pass from one of her team unless it is touched by an opponent, or unless one of own team with the puck is between her and the opponents' goal. The penalty for off-side play is facing the ball where the foul occurred. This rule does not hold in defense directly in front of the goal. One point is scored when the puck passes between the goal posts lower than their highest point.

The teams change goals to begin the second half.

The fouls are:

To lift the stick above the shoulder except when lifting the puck.

To throw a stick.

To hit, trip, or block a player by holding the stick in a horizontal position.

To body check or charge from behind, to trip, kick, push, hold with hand or stick.

For the goal keeper to sit, kneel, or lie.

To grasp, carry, or push the puck with any part of the body.

To interfere with a player not in possession of the puck.

The penalty for a foul is: The offender may be ruled off the ice for a certain time.

Officials.

There is a referee who controls the game and inflicts the penalties.

There are two umpires, one at each end, to decide whether a goal has been made. There are two timekeepers to keep the time of the game and a penalty timekeeper who keeps the time of players ruled out and notifies the player when she may return to the game.

There is for each team a captain, who makes the decisions for her team, and she is responsible for the good sportsmanship of her team.

There are many little tricks in ice hockey that may be acquired with practice, but the object of the game should be to have as clean and fast a game as possible, where skillful playing holds greater sway than roughness.

ROWING

The stroke; racing; paddling.

Very lucky is the school or college that has the necessary facilities for rowing. Wherever this form of sport is indulged in, it is generally popular. It deserves its popularity, for not only is it one of the most pleasant outdoor recreations but it is also very beneficial, since it brings into play practically all the muscles in the body.

In rowing, as in other sports, there is a great difference between competitive and non-competitive work. Whether racing or merely taking a pleasure row, the stroke is, however, fundamentally the same.

First, the position in the boat is to be considered. The oarsman sits in the center of the boat with her back toward the bow, facing the stern, with her feet planted firmly on the bottom of the boat, knees bent, slightly apart. An oar is grasped firmly in each hand, the oars having previously been adjusted in the oar-locks. There is a difference in the racing stroke, as shown under Racing.

Position of the Hands on the Oar.—Next to be considered is the stroke itself. The blade of the oar is just above the water and perpendicular to it. The arms and hands are straight, so that the hands holding the oars are just above the toes.

Catch.—Then the blades enter the water, turned forward so that they are held in the water vertically. The body is then swung backward from the hips; all the strength and weight of the body are put to the oars.

Pull.—As the body is swinging backward, the arms are bent into the chest. The blade of the oar is kept under water during the entire length of the pull.

Recovery.—As the hands touch the chest, the forearm is dropped quickly, thus causing the blade to leave the water.

Feathering.—The blade is carried a few inches above and horizontal to the water. It is gradually turned, as the catch is reached, to a perpendicular position, ready to enter the water as the arms are straightened ready for the catch.

Legs.—Where a sliding seat is used the object is to combine the use of the arms and legs in making the sweep of the oar longer, at full reach the body being doubled up with the knees under the chin, the stroke consisting of catching the water with the back and forcing it through to the finish by combined action of back and legs. When the finish is reached the legs are straight, the hands and oar are against the chest, and the body slightly back of the perpendicular.

Racing

The racing stroke is the same, except that for the four and eight-oared crews each oarsman pulls one oar, known as a "sweep," holding it in both hands—the inside hand at the end of the oar, the outside hand a hand's breadth away. The boats used for racing are known as "shells," especially made for the purpose. These have sliding seats and are equipped with either oar-locks or thole pins (according to the belief of the coach) and stretchers, or boards against which the feet rest. When the body is forward, the sliding seat is forward toward the bow; as the pull is starting, the seat comes back until the body is back, then it moves forward as body swings forward.

In racing, the shell is steered by a coxswain, who sits in the stern facing the oarsmen and holds the lines which guide the rudder. This is very important, since she tries to choose the best and most favorable course. She must observe all conditions closely. She alters the course as little as possible, taking care not to jerk or in any way interfere with running of the boat. She also judges the stroke, that is, when the stroke should be faster or slower.

The stroke oar is the most important position in the boat, since all the others time their strokes according to *hers*, either faster or slower, according to the necessity.

Above everything necessary in racing is a good coach, who watches carefully for any signs of fatigue or over-exertion. It never pays in the long run to overdo. The crew should work smoothly, harmoniously and with perfect mastery of the stroke. This can be obtained through the supervision of the coach, who criticises the individual and the whole. In arranging a crew the heavier girls are in the center, the lighter at either end; the coxswain should be as small and light as possible, thus not adding much unused weight.

In the single and double sculls—that is, boats rowed by one or two oarsmen—an oar is grasped in each hand. The sculler steers by pulling evenly on both oars for a straight course, or more strongly on one or the other oar for a variation of the course.

Rules for Racing.

Boat races, or regattas, are held on fixed courses for measured distances. In choosing a course, the natural and local conditions have to be considered. The most desirable are straightaway over inland waters with no, or little, current. If the course is in tidal water, the race should be so timed that it is not necessary for the crew to row against the tide.

The start and the finish are marked by flags. The stern must be on a line with the start. The bow first crossing the finish line wins. A tie is usually rowed over again.

The start is generally made at the pistol shot, fired by the official starter. Each boat has been assigned to a course, decided by lot. The winner has first choice and should make the most of the opportunity, considering position, tide, wind and other local conditions. No crew may go into another's course.

If the course is not straightaway, each boat must turn around the turning stake in its own course.

Besides an official starter, there is an umpire who judges the races; a judge or judges of the finish.

The different kinds of crews are: Single—one oarsman; doubles—two oarsmen, each pulling two oars; pairs—two oarsmen each pulling one oar; fours—four oarsmen each with one oar; eights—each with one oar.

Paddling

Closely allied to rowing is paddling. This is done in a canoe by one, two, or more people. If by one, she seats herself in the stern, facing the bow; if two, one is in the stern and one is in the bow, back toward the stern. There are rarely more than three or four in a canoe, the average being two people to a canoe.

The Indians of the Canadian backwoods usually delegate the responsibility of steering to the bow man because of rough water or the danger from submerged rocks in swift running streams. Usually, in more civilized waters, the steering is done by the paddler in the stern, who, by a twist of the wrists, turns the blade of the paddle toward the canoe or away, according to the direction desired. The paddle is held in both hands; the near hand is held pretty far down the blade, more than shoulder's width from far hand, which is held over the top of the paddle. There are many forms of paddling; some prefer straight, others bent arms. The reach with the paddle should not be so far ahead of the paddler that she is forced to lean forward. The paddle is brought out of the water when both arms are straight back, body in a normal position. It is carried forward but a few inches above the water with blade flat.

An Indian custom that has come down to us is the double paddle. The paddle is fashioned with a handle in the middle and paddles at either end. The paddler sits in the center of the canoe. First the paddle is dipped in the water at the left and then to the right. Steering is done by turning the paddle, in or out, as you would go, left or right. The double paddle is fascinating, but hardly so safe for the novice as the single.

Practice and experience are the two best teachers.

Rowing is eagerly participated in by the girls at Wellesley College. The formation of the star shows how proficient they have become in handling the oars.

The tennis enthusiast will not admit there is a more fascinating, healthful or elevating sport in the whole world. Wellesley College provides plenty of tennis courts and the setting is ideal.

TENNIS

The court; the game; matches or tournaments.

Tennis scarcely needs an introduction. It is one of the finest games—for girls or men—we have, and it has proved its worth through years and years of play.

Tennis is played on a rectangular court, either of turf, clay or cement, provided that it is level. The dimensions of the court for doubles are 36 by 78 feet. The 78-foot lines are known as the side lines; the others as the end or base lines. Parallel to each base line and 18 feet distant from are two service lines, drawn from side service line to side service line. Parallel to each side line and 4½ feet distant from them is a side service line, drawn from end line to end line. A line exactly in center joins the two service lines, thus making four service courts. The net is stretched exactly across the center of the court, and should be 3 feet high in the middle. It is desirable that there be no obstructions within 3 feet of the court on the side and 12 feet at ends, and that there should be backstops of considerable height. The posts to which net is attached should be 3 feet away from the court.

The game may be played by two, three or four players, who bat a ball across the net with a racket until one or the other fails to return the ball. If only two play (or, as it is termed, "singles"), the side lines are dispensed with and the side service lines are the boundary lines (27 × 78 feet).

The ball is put in play by the server. The courts and service are determined by a toss; the winner may choose either the end of court or the serve, but not both. The server, standing on the right-hand side of her base line, with feet behind the line, sends the ball into her opponent's right-hand court. The player receiving ball after it has bounced must return it over the net so that it touches inside the court; then the server returns, etc., until there is a failure to return the ball. This counts a point for opposing player of the one who makes the fault. Then the ball is again served, this time from the left-hand side, next from the right, continuing to alternate until the game is finished. A game is always begun by serving from the right-hand court.

The game is won when a player has scored four points, except in the case of deuce, when more are necessary. The first point is "15;" the second, "30;" the third, "40;" the fourth, "game." If both players have "15," it is "15-all;" if one, "15-love (or naught)." The server's score is always called first. If both have 30, 30-all; if one has 30, the other none or 15, it is 30-love, or 30-15. If both have 40, it is "deuce." In deuce it is necessary to play extra points. The first point won is "advantage in" (server) or "out" (striker), as may be the case; the next point if won by the same player is game, but if won by the other player it is deuce again, and so on until one player wins two points in succession.

The server, after the first game, becomes the receiver, and the serve is alternated with each game until the end of the set. A set consists of six games won by one player, unless the opposing player is less than two games behind, that is, a set cannot end at 6/5, but must be played until one or the other obtains a two-game lead. Ends of the court are exchanged after each set. The server should always keep the score.

It is the aim of the players to return as many good balls as possible. A ball is "good" when it is sent within the court. It is a "fault" when it hits outside the boundary lines, or does not clear the net—a ball, however, which touches net but still falls on the right side (a "let ball") is "good." Faults count one point for opponent or opponents. Other faults that count for opponent are: Server serves two faults in succession; volleying the ball before it has touched the net; volleying a served ball before it bounds (any other ball may be volleyed); failure to return a ball. It is a fault to touch net while ball is in play, or to touch the ball with any part of person except the racket, or to touch ball with racket twice.

The receiver may hit the ball in the air (except serve) or after the first bounce, but may never hit after the second bounce.

A player in tennis must never be caught napping. Tennis calls for wide awake, quick playing. It is best to stand either near the net or back farther toward the service line. For most girls I would recommend the base line game. Never stand where your opponent can drop a ball directly at your feet; always be ready for her. You must always watch where she is and try to place the ball in the spot most difficult for her to reach.

In order to be ready the racket should be held firmly and easily so that it may be prepared for any stroke. Above all, keep your eye on the ball; if you look at the place you want to hit the ball and not at the ball, you do not hit it squarely and you give your play away. When you receive, do not stand too far away or too near. If you are too far away, you are apt to tip it; if too near, you bend your arm and do not get a good stroke.

The game of tennis is divided into two main divisions, serving and receiving. First, let us take up serving. This is the method of putting the ball in play. The server must stand behind the base line of the court. She must serve her ball into the diagonally opposite service court. She is allowed two balls; if the first is a fault she is allowed to serve the second. To be a good ball it must touch the ground in the service court, fairly clearing the net. A double fault on the part of the server counts a point for the opposing side, that is, it is a fault to serve two balls which do not clear the net, or do not touch inside the service court. When the ball touches the net but goes into the proper service court, it is called a "let ball" and does not count, but is served over again. Failure to return the ball after it is served counts one point for the server. The server must not step across the base line while serving, nor must she step, hop, walk or run.

In serving it is important to study the grip of the racket, the method of hitting the ball, and the way to toss the ball into the air. The racket is held tightly in the hand by what is known as the long grip, hand at the end of the racket—usually the right hand. There are many different swings and twists used. It is best to adopt one that brings into play the full strength of the arm and shoulder, thus an overhead swing of the racket is most often used. The ball is tossed into the air and the racket, in its exact center, should hit the ball directly over the net into the opposite service court. Before a cut or a speedier serve is developed, the player should make sure of a steady ball that as a rule is good. After that is acquired, practice the cuts and put as much speed as possible into the serve. It is very important that the ball and the racket should meet at the psychological moment. If the ball is hit too low, it does not clear the net; if it is hit while too high in the air, it goes out of the service court. The follow through of the stroke should be natural and never chopped.

In receiving and returning the ball there are many different strokes to use. It is advisable for the beginner to perfect both forehand and backhand strokes. For these strokes, the racket should be held in the short grip, that is, the end of the racket is at the wrist, hand reaching up the handle; the forearm should be in a line with the racket.

One stroke, the drop stroke, the arm is back of the body, extended to full length; then move—rather sweep—forward to meet the ball as it is about waist high, giving a little upward turn to your racket. Always follow through. The arm should be straight in this stroke.

Besides a forehand stroke, a backhand stroke is also necessary to learn. In the forehand, the weight is on the right foot, but in the backhand it is on the left foot. There are many different kinds, but the most natural is the best for the beginner to use. The arm and racket, of course, are across the body. Swing back and meet the ball squarely, with body turned greatly to that side. Be careful to follow through.

A great many people spoil their game of tennis by wild playing and smashes. It is much better to be deliberate and calculating, carefully placing your shots out of reach of your opponent. Try to make every play count. In other words, use your head rather than brute strength.

A good racket—carefully chosen for weight and balance and to which you have become accustomed—practice, a deliberate study of the game and your playing—these will help the average player.

The most suitable dress for tennis is a light weight waist or a middy blouse; a short, wide skirt, and rubber or felt-soled flat-heeled shoes.

Tennis Matches or Tournaments.

For a tennis match there should be an official referee, who determines questions concerning the rules; an umpire, who judges all balls except those on the lines, which are judged by the linesmen; a linesman for each of the seven lines, whose duty it is to judge the ball near her line. There may be a scorer, but this duty is generally assumed by the umpire, who announces each point, the score of each game, and how the sets stand.

Each player should enter her name in advance; then each draws for opponent, the winner of one match meeting the winner of another, etc., until the final match is played. This is an elimination tournament. In doubles, the pair may be entered or the partner may be drawn for.

A favorite form of tournament where the number of entrants is small is the round robin tournament, where each contestant meets every other, irrespective of victories. The championship with its trophy is given to the girl winning the greatest number of matches.

Tournament play is greatly to be recommended, especially for schools or clubs. Match play adds considerably to the pleasure of the sport and usually has beneficial results, both physical and physiological. I have seen diffident girls taught to gain self control and composure at all times by competitive athletics. A tennis tournament can be made a gala social event as well as one of keen and interesting sport.

CRICKET

The game; as played at Smith College.

Cricket is not widely played by girls, but there is no game which might be adopted to better advantage. It may be played without any danger of over-exertion. A cricket crease may be placed on any level grassy field, usually a ground 100 yards square, although a smaller field may be utilized. The equipment required includes two sets of wickets, a cricket ball, at least two bats, the wicket-keeper gloves and leg guards, and a leg guard for each of two batsmen who are in. There are eleven players on each team and the game is divided into innings; that is, a side has its inning when it is at the bat. Two batsmen are "in" at a time.

The wickets are set in the middle of the field, opposite, parallel and 22 yards apart. On a line with the wicket is the bowling crease, 8 feet 8 inches in length. Four feet in front and parallel to it is the popping crease, of unlimited length.

The batsman who is first striker takes her position with bat on the popping crease, the bowler at the opposite wicket, well behind bowling crease; also the second batsman, bat in hand, ready to run when hit is made. The bowler delivers the ball. It must be bowled, not thrown, tossed, or jerked. The bowler is allowed a run in her delivery, but she must keep one foot on the ground behind the bowling crease and within the return crease, otherwise it is no ball.

The bowler must deliver the ball so that it shall come to the batsman on the ground. If it is delivered high or wide, the umpire shall call "wide ball." Six good balls make an "over;" the bowler shall be allowed to change ends when she pleases, provided she has not bowled two "overs" consecutively in one inning. The captain of the outs places the field as she deems wise, depending upon the skill of the batsman.

The striker hits the ball; if it is caught before it touches the ground she is out; if the wicket is knocked down by a bowled ball she is out. If she hits it safe she runs to the return crease and the other batsman runs to the opposite popping crease and a run is scored. If the hit is long enough the batsmen continue to run, and each time they exchange creases a run is counted. The fielders endeavor to get the ball and throw in to the wicket-keeper in order to knock off the bails before the batsman touches her bat to the ground within the crease. When the bail is knocked off in this manner the batsman is out. When a batsman is out for any cause she is retired for the inning, and the side is retired when ten of the eleven strikers are declared out.

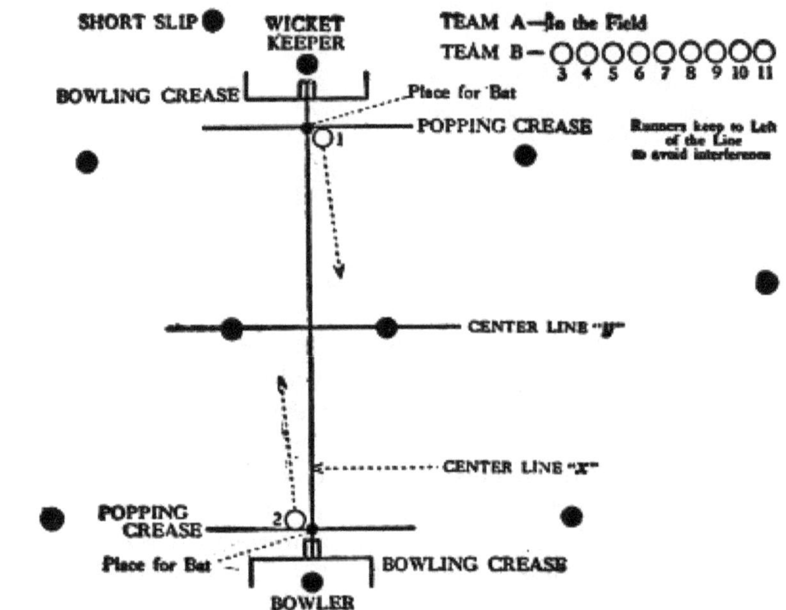

DIAGRAM OF FIELD OF PLAY.

SCORING SHEET						=5 Runs	=Out
TEAM A	1	2	3	TEAM B	1	2	3
1				1			
2				2			
3				3			
4				4			
5				5			
6				6			
7				7			
8				8			
9				9			
10				10			
11				11			
RUNS	2	2	2	RUNS	2	2	2
No Balls and Wides				No Balls and Wides			
Bowler B				Bowler A			
Bowler B				Bowler A			
TOTAL				TOTAL			
Good Balls	(Six Good Balls is a "Bowling Over")			Good Balls			
Bowler B				Bowler A			
Bowler B				Bowler A			
Add Total Scores at end of 3d Inning				Add Total Scores at end of 3d Inning			

SAMPLE SCORING SHEET.

Usually in the matches for girls only one inning for each team is played, although the rules call for two and three-day matches. The game affords ample opportunity for outdoor exercise and muscular activity. For a full description, see Spalding's "How to Play Cricket."

Cricket has been successfully played by girls. Miss Dorothy Wooster writes the following short article and gives a diagram and score card showing how the game is played at Smith College.

Cricket as Played at Smith College
By Dorothy Wooster.

In order to adapt cricket for practical use, the following additions and changes have been made in the official rules, as published in the Spalding Athletic Library.

A. Additions:

1. Diagram of Field: Use center line, "*x*," drawn between wickets. Cross this line by another line, "*y*," drawn parallel to the popping crease.

2. There shall be 3 innings to a game, each inning consisting of 3 "outs" on a side.

3. There shall be a definite batting order.

4. If a batter touches the ball with the bat she must run, or take her "out."

B. Changes in Rules:

10. ... and to be a good ball, the ball must hit the ground on or across the center line "*y*."

13. A "Bowling Over" shall consist of six "good balls," or four "wide balls," or four "no balls."

33A. ... except in case of a "Caught Ball." The ball is then in play until it is settled in bowler's or wicket-keeper's hand. This change gives an opportunity to put two runners out on one play; i. e., "Caught Out" and "Run Out."

The scoring has been simplified. For practice games, when full teams are not present, an individual score is kept. Using these changes the game progresses rapidly and holds the interest of both players and spectators.

SOCCER

The game; rules.

Soccer or association football is a particularly suitable game for girls and women, since it furnishes splendid outdoor exercise without unnecessary roughness. It resembles field hockey in that it is mainly a running game, although there are many essential differences. The popularity of the game is rapidly increasing and it is played by many schools and colleges.

The game is primarily a running and kicking game. No player but the goal keeper in her own goal area is permitted to touch the ball with the hands. Two teams of eleven players each line up in their half of the field. The captains toss for the choice of end or for the choice of the kick-off. In making the choice, the wind and the position of the sun should be considered. The ball is put in play by a kick-off. To advance the ball to the opponents' goal and to kick the ball between the goal posts and under the bar is the object of the game. Each goal counts one. The team having the highest score at the end of the two halves—time of which is determined by the captains—is the winner. Thus the two opposing teams are either attacking or defending. If one side has possession of the ball it should advance toward the opponents' goal, thus attacking; if the ball is not in their possession they are checking their opponents' advance, thus defending. The players who do most of the attacking are the five forwards, assisted by the halfbacks. It is their duty to advance the ball by short and long passes, by dribbling, by a volley, i. e., hitting the ball with head or chest, or kicking it before it has touched the ground. The fullbacks and goal keeper, assisted by the halfbacks, do the defensive work.

The positions are: center forward, inside right and inside left, outer right and outer left; left, center, and right halfbacks; right and left fullbacks; goal keeper.

The beginner in soccer should pay particular attention to the following: kicking, tackling, heading, and dribbling. The ball is not kicked with the end of toe, but rather the toe is inserted under the ball, the instep bearing the brunt of the work. The leg should be drawn back to get a good drive. Kicking is not merely sending the ball as far and hard as possible, but kicking as accurately as possible so that each shot tells. Therefore, particular attention and practice should be given to kicking until the proper amount of control can be exercised over the ball. Every kick should be gotten off quickly and cleanly, toe well under the ball so that it is raised.

In shooting for the goal the kick should be hard, with all the force of the toe behind it. In all defensive work the kicks should be carefully sent to the forwards; not too hard, since the ball then may go too far.

The player should learn to kick with either foot so that the ball does not have to be maneuvered into a suitable position for kicking.

Every player—the forwards in particular—should know how to dribble, since it is frequently a handy art. Often, if a player wishes to get in a better position for a kick, a few dribbles will put her there. To dribble successfully, the ball is moved forward, just touching the toe, thus insuring complete control. For the inexperienced player, control in dribbling and speed seem a hard combination to achieve; but by practice, dribbling slowly at first, control is acquired and speed soon follows.

A common fault sometimes due to dribbling is the monopoly of the ball by one player. Any individual should be self-sacrificing for the good of the team.

Stopping the progress of an opponent, or "tackling" as it is termed, should be carefully practised, particularly by the defense. The best policy seems—to run directly toward the player with the ball, thus making her pass hurriedly or fumble. Never give up if your opponent gets away, dodges or slips past you.

Many times it is an advantage to "head" the ball, that is, hit it with the head before it touches the ground. When the players are massed together, a jump in the air and good "heading" may save the day. Remember that the ball ought to be hit with the forehead, not the top of the head. This makes for accuracy.

There should be, as in all other team games, team work. The forwards should bear the responsibility of the attack. They should carry the ball down the field by passing, dribbling and volleying, i. e., hitting the ball in the air before it has touched the ground. Forwards should know how to shoot hard and accurately. It is well for a forward to know how to shoot and pass with the inside of the foot. In dribbling and in passing, the forward must remember to pass quickly to some one of her team who is unguarded. You should always be waiting to receive a pass.

The outsides are generally fast players with great skill in the dribble; the insides, like the center, are fine offensive players, fast and capable of shooting goals.

The halfbacks feed and help the forwards attack, shooting for the goal if the opportunity arises. The attack should be constantly varied by these players. The halfbacks are also the first line of defense, necessarily they have a great deal of running to do. These three positions are generally filled then by players physically fit, with speed and with stamina for endurance. Center half is a particularly strenuous position. The halves should always try to keep the ball in the opponents' territory; when on the defense, they should be quick to tackle, to intercept passes and to guard their opponents.

The fullbacks are the mainstay of the defense. They are cool-headed players who use great judgment. It is up to them to block any opponent who has gotten by a halfback. Often the fullbacks have so carefully studied their opponents' play that they know exactly what the forward will do under certain circumstances. Above all, the fullbacks should never give up.

The goal is a very vital point. To be a goal keeper, you must think quickly, keep your nerve, be cool and act instantly according to your judgment. In fact, a goal keeper should be able to cover every inch of the goal in an instant; she must be able to move rapidly, jump, and reach into the air. Two points a goal keeper should remember: Never kick when you can use your hands—you can get rid of the ball quicker and for better distance. Get the ball out of dangerous territory as soon as possible.

Cricket—Well hit! A good free swing with the ball well met often means a "boundary."

Soccer is a splendid action game. The forward is well up on the ball while the fullback is coming up fast.

Dress is an important consideration. The essentials are a middy blouse, a short, wide skirt or bloomers, with heavy enough shoes to allow for kicking and yet light enough to permit of speed in covering ground.

Soccer Rules.

[From Spalding's Athletic Library No. 358—Official College Soccer Guide.]

I. There are eleven players on a team.

II. The field of play is a quadrangle. Its dimensions vary from 130 to 100 yards in length and from 100 to 50 yards in breadth. A smaller field, as near these dimensions as possible, may be used. The lines, areas, etc., do not vary with any change in size of the field, however. Flags on five-foot staffs are placed at each of the four corners. The lines are distinctly marked with whitewash if possible. The quadrangle is bounded by two end or "goal" lines and two side or "touch" lines which are at right angles with the goal lines. The field is exactly halved by a cross line. In the center of the field of play is a circle with a ten-yard radius. The goals are marked by goal posts, eight feet apart, in the middle of the goal line, equidistant from the side lines. The posts are joined by a cross-bar eight feet from the ground, and neither the posts nor cross-bar are more than five inches in width. At each end of the field in front of the goal is a goal area. Lines are marked six yards from each goal post at right angles to the goal line, extending in field for six yards. These two lines are connected by a line parallel to the goal line. The enclosed space is a goal area.

There is also a penalty area in front of each goal. Lines are marked 18 yards from each goal post at right angles to the goal lines, extending in field for a distance of 18 yards. These two lines are joined by a line parallel to the goal lines.

A mark 12 yards distant from and opposite the exact center of each goal designates the penalty kick mark.

The ball should be a regulation association football.

III. The game is divided into two halves, each 45 minutes long, with an interval of five minutes between the halves unless a different length of time is agreed upon by the captains. Ends are changed at half time.

IV. The choice of end or kick-off is decided by the toss of a coin. The game is started by a place-kick, i. e., the ball is placed on the ground and kicked from this position in the center of the field. All opponents are more than ten yards away; no player may cross center of the ground until the ball is kicked. After a goal is scored the ball is kicked off by the team which did not score the goal. At the beginning of the second half the ball is kicked by the opposing side from the side that kicked first.

V. A goal is scored when the ball passes between the goal posts under the bar, provided that it has not been thrown, knocked, or carried.

VI. When the ball goes out of bounds over the touch line, a player of the opposite side from that playing it out, throws it in. She must stand on the touch line facing the field of play; the ball may be thrown in any direction, provided it is thrown over the head with both hands. A goal may not be scored from a throw-in. The thrower-in may not touch the ball until it has been touched by another player.

When the ball goes out of bounds over the goal line, played over by an attacker, it is kicked off by a defender, within the half of the goal area nearest the point where the ball went out. If it was sent out by a defender, it is kicked by an attacker from a point within one yard of nearest corner flag. No player in either case may be within 10 yards of the ball until the kick-off is taken.

VII. If, after the ball has been played or thrown in, it is touched by a player on the same side as the person last touching it, who at the moment of playing is nearer her opponents' goal than the person last playing the ball, she is off-side and may not interfere with the ball or opponent. *She is not offside,* however, if at the time of play there are at least three of her opponents between her and the goal, or if she is within her own half of the field, or in a corner kick, or if the ball was last touched by an opponent.

VIII. The goal keeper may use her hands to catch or to throw the ball if she is within her own penalty area.

IX. There should be no tripping, kicking, striking, jumping at, handling (except in Rule VI), holding, pushing, obstructing, or charging from behind. The goal keeper may be charged if she is holding the ball, or obstructing or outside her own goal area. The penalty for a foul is a free kick.

X. A free kick is taken for any infringement of a rule. The ball must roll over—travel the distance of its circumference—to be considered played. No opponent may stand within 10 yards unless standing on own goal line. The kicker may not touch the ball a second time until it has been touched by another player. A goal may be scored from a free kick if it is granted for any breaking of Rule VII.

XI. Any intentional infringement by either the attackers or defenders outside the penalty area, a free kick is awarded to opposing side.

If, however, there is an intentional foul by the defenders within the penalty area, a penalty kick is granted to the opposing side. All players except the goal keeper and a player from the opposing side who is to take the kick remain outside the penalty area. The goal keeper must not advance beyond the goal line. The ball is kicked forward and a goal may be scored from a penalty kick. The ball must be kicked and may not be touched again by the kicker until it has been touched by another player.

XII. There is a referee who controls the game and enforces the rules. Her power in the game is supreme. The ball is in play until the decision is given.

There are two linesmen who decide when the ball is out of play, what player has the corner kick, goal kick, or throw-in.

The referee acts as timekeeper.

To restart the game stopped temporarily, the referee drops the ball to the ground on the spot where it was when play was suspended. The ball is in play when it touches the ground.

ARCHERY

The bow and arrow; the aim and draw; games; tournament; score; clubs.

Archery might be classed as a pioneer sport for women. The art of the bow and arrow has been exploited ever since the written records of man. At the present time, when such sports as basket ball, field hockey, track athletics, etc., are the popular games, archery has been less in favor. There is no reason why any athletic girl who can run the hundred in good time, and acquit herself creditably in any of the more strenuous sports, should smile a supercilious smile at *Archery*—mere child's play in her mind. In fact, it is far from child's play, and it has all the advantages of wholesome outdoor competition.

In order to be successful at archery two things are necessary—perseverance and a trained eye. Any girl without particular athletic ability can learn how to hold the bow and take aim. Both requisites may be acquired through practice. There is no need for great strength or for any violent exertion. It is particularly good for growing girls where more violent exercise might be harmful.

The archer should look first to her bow, which should be neither too heavy nor too strong. A beginner should not use a bow that is heavy. The bow together with the arrow should be tested and if it can be raised and drawn without strain it has the proper weight. Another point to be considered is steadiness; no bow should kick or jar after the string is released.

The arrows should also be chosen carefully according to weight and length. An arrow that is too heavy will weaken the bow; an arrow that is too light will not fly truly. Arrows vary in length and should be chosen according to length of arm, so that when the arrow is drawn the proper form can be maintained. A right-handed archer extends the left arm full length holding the bow, while the right hand (grasping the string with the notch of the arrow adjusted) should be at the right cheek; therefore the length of the arrow should be governed by the length of the left arm.

Bows vary from three feet to five feet six inches and arrows from fifteen inches to twenty-five inches. The arrows should be carefully kept when not in use. A quiver and belt is a desirable added equipment. Some archers find a bracer or arm guard necessary.

In shooting the arrow the first consideration is the position of standing. The side of body should be directly toward the target (or the point aimed at), the head turned toward the target, looking over the shoulder. The feet—heels slightly apart—should be at right angles to an imaginary line drawn directly from target.

Next to be considered is nocking the arrow. The bow should be held in a horizontal position, the arrow is laid across the bow and the nock or notch of the arrow is fitted on the string by the right hand.

The position of the hand is important. The string is held by three fingers, the string resting near the tips of the fingers above the first joint; the arrow rests between the first and second fingers; the thumb and little finger should not touch the arrow or the string.

Next comes the draw. Raise the bow hand, drawing on the string slightly; take a preliminary sight; then the draw is taken almost the full distance, the full aim is caught, and the arrow is released when drawn to the fullest extent. Another way is to raise the bow, draw to the fullest extent, take aim by moving the hand on the bow handle up or down as the need dictates; loose the string by straightening the fingers while the hand is drawn entirely back.

The archer should never shoot more than three arrows in succession without resting. The fourth and succeeding flights are apt to be inaccurate if the arms are the least bit tired. Always be sure to shoot every arrow carefully—never hurry.

The bows and arrows should be well taken care of. They should be cleaned and wiped thoroughly after each use. Never use a blunt arrow; it will not hold in the target. The bow should always be unstrung after it is used and strung before using again.

The arrow should be uniformly nocked at the same point upon the string in order to insure accuracy. Thus, it is desirable to wrap the string at the proper point with a different colored thread.

Games.

The most ancient form of archery is the so-called roving game, which consists of roving about and shooting at marks from various distances. Another form is flight shooting—seeking to cast an arrow the greatest possible distance.

Modern archery, however, is practically confined to target shooting. A target is a flat disc, varying from eighteen inches to forty-eight inches in diameter. It is marked by concentric rings or bands of different colors. From center to the outer ring the colors are gold, red, blue, black, and white; the latter is usually banded by a narrow strip of green. The dimensions are: gold nine and six-tenths inches, and the width of each of the other rings is exactly half that amount.

Tournament.

The archer standing at a prescribed distance shoots at the target, trying to make as many hits as possible and to place the arrows in the gold. Three arrows are usually shot at a time, then three more. The six arrows form an end. A given number of ends form a range, while two or three ranges form a round.

The Score.

A hit is counted if the arrow pierces the target. The values of the different bands are: gold, 9; red, 7; blue, 5; black, 3; white, 1. An arrow cutting or touching the line between rings counts for the higher value. Also one hit is counted if the arrow rebounds from face of or if it passes through the body of the target; this adds one point to the score.

The Rounds for Ladies are:

I.—National Round.

48 arrows at 60 yards.
24 arrows at 50 yards.

At the double of this the National Championship is decided.

II.—Columbia Round.

24 arrows at 50 yards.
24 arrows at 40 yards.
24 arrows at 30 yards.

The Ladies' Interclub team and mid-range matches are contested with 96 arrows at 50 yards.

Archery Clubs.

The sport of archery gives a splendid opportunity for the formation of clubs with weekly or bi-weekly tournaments. Groups of girls can adopt a color designating teams where there are no other means of rivalry; thus, team and individual trophies may be contested for.

The grounds for archery should be carefully chosen. The most suitable ground is a level, grassy space with a uniform background. It is well to see that no danger can come to anyone through a flying arrow.

Soccer at Wellesley College before a large gallery. Soccer is a growing sport in America and an exceedingly healthful one.

Archery: 1, A target match at 50 yards. 2, The firing line, showing "nocked" arrows and drawn bows. 3, Retrieving arrows and counting scores. 4, A close up showing good form in "nocking" the arrow and drawing the bow.

INDOOR BASE BALL

The game; rules.

Indoor base ball, like basket ball, is a game that may be played in the winter months in the gymnasium and it may also be played outdoors in a comparatively small space. When well played, it may become as exciting as the outdoor game. Its similarity to the outdoor game makes it easier for a majority of the players to understand it quickly. The ball is pitched by a pitcher to a batter who tries to hit it, in order to run to first base. Each batter in turn tries to advance her teammates and herself so that they each may touch each of the four bases in turn, thus making a run. There are nine innings. In each inning each team has a turn at bat, or an opportunity to bring in runs. The three main points are batting, pitching and fielding.

The pitcher throws the ball with a straight arm and with an underarm throw. Of course, she endeavors to find the batter's weak spots and pitch accordingly. The fewer hits made by the batter, the greater the glory of the pitcher.

The batter must use common sense, and not let the pitcher fool her. To make every hit count is the rule for the batter; thus she must judge the ball, hit to a favorable spot in the field, working with the object of advancing such of her teammates already on the bases. The base runner should always be wideawake, ready to take advantage of any opportunities offered to her.

The fielders must be quick to judge a ball, quick to catch it, and throw immediately to the necessary spot to head off any incipient scoring by a base runner.

A quick, well-played game of indoor base ball is lots of fun.

Indoor Base Ball Rules.

THE DIAMOND OR INFIELD.

The game is played on an indoor floor. The diamond or infield is marked out at one end, the remaining floor is the outfield. At each of the four corners of the diamond is a base, usually made of canvas and half filled with sand. The distance along the sides is 27 feet if possible. There should be a box for the pitcher, 7 by 3 feet, and 23 feet distant from center of home base. A batsman's box, one on each side of the home base, six inches distant from the base. The boxes are each 4 by 3 and extend a foot in front of a line drawn through center of the base and 3 feet behind. Foul lines should be drawn from the home base to first and from third to home, outside the side lines, so that the bases are inside the foul lines.

THE BALL AND BAT.

The regulation indoor base ball and bat are used.

THE PLAYERS.

There may be seven to nine players on a side, placed in position by the captain. There must be one player who stands within the pitcher's box and pitches the ball according to rule. A substitute may be put in to run for a player by consent of both captains.

THE GAME.

The game has nine innings for each side. If there is a tie the game is continued by innings until one side has won, or game is discontinued. Choice of innings is decided by the toss of a coin.

THE SCORE.

One run, i. e., one point to the side making the run, is scored when a base runner runs to and touches each of the three bases and touches home base before three players of her side are out.

THE PITCHER.

The pitcher delivers the ball with the arm parallel to the body. The pitcher may not take more than one step.

THE BALL.

The ball is good if it passes over any portion of the home plate no lower than the batsman's knee and no higher than her shoulder.

It is counted a balk by the pitcher if she makes any motion to deliver the ball without doing so or holds the ball so long as to delay the game.

An illegal ball is delivered by the pitcher if she steps out of box or takes more than one step while pitching that ball.

A dead ball is a pitched ball which strikes the batter.

A batted ball is fair unless it strikes outside the foul line first.

A blocked ball is a ball batted or thrown that is stopped or handled by a person not playing. The ball is returned to the pitcher and runners remain on the same bases.

A strike is:

1. A ball struck at by the batter without her touching it.
2. A foul tip caught.
3. A good ball, legally delivered by the pitcher, not struck at by the batter.
4. A good ball which the batter deliberately interferes with.

A foul strike is a ball batted when the batter is out of her position.

The batsman is out:

1. If she bats out of turn.

2. If she fails to take her position one minute after umpire calls for batter.

3. If a foul hit made by her is caught by the catcher before the ball touches the floor or the wall.

4. If she makes a foul strike.

5. If any attempt be made to hinder the catcher or if the ball is intentionally fouled.

6. If, first base being occupied by a base runner, the batter has three strikes, except when two players are already out.

7. If, on the third strike, she is hit by the ball. The base runner must touch in regular order first, second, third and home bases.

The batter is a base runner immediately after:

1. A fair hit.

2. Four balls.

3. Three strikes.

4. Illegal delivery by pitcher.

The player is granted one base for the above, also the player may advance one base if:

1. Succeeding player is granted a base.

2. If umpire is struck by a batted or thrown ball.

3. If she is prevented from making a base by an adversary.

If the ball is fumbled on the third strike or fourth ball the base runner may take as many bases as she can get.

The base runner may only leave her base when the ball has been struck, or, if it is not struck, it has reached the catcher.

The base runner is brought back if:

1. She starts too soon.

2. For a foul strike.

3. A dead ball.

4. A foul hit not legally fielded. The pitcher must wait for her to return.

The base runner is out:

1. If having made a fair hit, this is fielded before it touches the wall or floor.

2. If there is any intentional interference with the ball just batted.

3. If the third strike is caught before touching the ground.

4. If, after three strikes or a fair hit, the base runner before touching first base is touched by a fielder with the ball in her hands, or if the ball is securely held by fielder touching first base before the base runner touches first base.

5. If she does not run directly.

6. If she obstructs the fielder.

7. If she fails to touch the bases in regular order.

The base runners may be coached from the coacher's box.

There are two umpires who control the game. One judges all balls, strikes, blocks, dead balls, balks, illegal deliveries, fair and foul hits, ground hits, foul strikes. All decisions at the home plate are made by her. Time and play are called. She stands in a position behind the catcher.

The other judges the base plays. She stands near base line where she can best see field of play.

The two change positions at the end of each inning.

A regulation score card should be used.

AMERICAN HAND BALL[1]

The game; rules.

Hand ball is a game suitable for either indoor or outdoor playing, in which two or four persons may participate. The game is divided into two parts—offensive and defensive. The server, or, if there are four playing, the server and her partner, constitute the offensive; the receiver or the receiving side, the defensive. The score is made by the serving side upon an error by the receiving side; if the server makes an error she loses the serve, thus also the chance to score. The ball is batted with the cupped hand against a wall or back board so that it bounds within a given territory.

The server drops or bounces the ball and then hits it on the rebound with the palm of hand against the wall, so that it rebounds as far from the receiver as possible. Control and speed are two important factors. In order to obtain good control, the player should practice and endeavor to place the ball where her opponent isn't. This requires careful observation of your opponent's tactics. After control comes speed; a speedy ball is always hard to return.

For the defensive, the player should always try to be in a good position to return any ball; thus, it is imperative to be able to play the ball with either hand. It is safer for the defensive player to play a conservative game rather than a speedy one, for any error counts for the other side.

Every player should learn to serve well, to use control and speed; every player should learn to become equally efficient with either hand, batting the ball with straight aim; every player should always remember to outmaneuver her opponent and place the ball where it is most difficult for her to return it.

Rules for American Hand Ball.

A hand ball court consists of a floor, a wall or back board, and field. The floor is usually 20 feet wide and 26 feet long, with a service line, distinctly marked, drawn across the floor at the middle point, 13 feet away, between the front line (end line 26 feet away from the board) and the board. The floor is smooth but not polished. The wall or back board is 10 feet high and 20 feet wide. The field is the whole space including the floor and is 55 feet wide and 40 feet long including the court.

A regulation hand ball (small hard-rubber ball hollow inside) and gloves are

[1] For further details see Spalding's "American Hand Ball."

used.

Points may only be scored by the side serving. Twenty-one points are a game. Should each score twenty points, either side must score two consecutive points on one serve to win.

There are two officials—a referee and an umpire—who have control of the game, who decide all questions of balls, time, unfair play, etc.

The choice of serving or receiving is decided by tossing a coin.

The ball is struck with the palm of either hand—one hand only—by no other part of body, nor by both hands simultaneously.

The ball is dropped or bounced to the floor by the server on that side of the service line farthest from the court. The served ball after touching the board must cross to the far side of the service line and land within the court. If it touches the floor on the near side of the service line, it is short; if it touches out of the court on the far side of the service line, it is long.

The server may serve these balls over again, but if one "short" and one "long;" or two "short" or two "long" balls are served consecutively by the same player, the server (or the side, if doubles) is out. Then the receiver becomes the server.

If a served ball touches the floor outside the side lines, the server or the side is out.

A served ball is played on the first bounce only. A returned ball may be played on the first bounce or on the fly. *All balls served or returned must touch the board before touching the floor.* A ball leaving the hand of a player striking opponent before touching wall or floor is a "hinder." Two hinders by one player in a service is a put-out or a point scored. A ball leaving the board which strikes the player who returned it, or partner, is a put-out or a point for the side struck. A ball leaving the board striking an opponent is a point or put-out in favor of the opposing side of person so struck.

All balls are played until decided by the referee.

A returned ball must be within the dimensions of the court.

Players may block each other fairly, that is, a player may so place the ball that he blocks his opponent, but this must be done before the ball has left his hand. In doubles, no blocking may be done after the ball has left the board.

For unfair blocking, a penalty—subtracting from one to five points from score of the offender—may be imposed by the referee.

In doubles, the sides alternate in service as well as receiving. No player shall serve or play the same defensive position all the time.

IRISH HAND BALL RULES

I. A ball may be batted with either hand.

Foul—Never with both hands.

Penalty—For server, loss of hand; for receiver, ace for server.

II. The server may stand anywhere in space between ace line and front line.

Foul—She must not step over inner line twice in succession while serving.

Penalty—Server loses hand.

III. A served ball must hit the front wall *before* it hits either side wall, roof or floor.

Foul—If served ball hits side wall, roof or floor before hitting front wall.

Penalty—Server loses hand.

IV. A served ball may be so played that after hitting front wall it rebounds from a side wall or the back wall, before touching the floor behind ace line.

V. Short ball.—If a served ball touches the floor inside the ace line (between that line and the front wall) it is called a short ball. Any number of short balls may be served with good balls in between.

Foul—To serve three short balls in succession.

Penalty—Server loses hand.

VI. If a short ball is served the receiver may or may not play according to her desire.

VII. A ball may never be batted or touched in any way twice by either server or receiver before it touches front wall.

Foul—To touch a ball twice in succession.

Penalty—Server loses hand; receiver, point to server.

VIII. If receiver fails to send back the ball to the front wall it counts ace for server. If server fails she is hand out.

IX. A server after retiring must be given time to get into position for receiving.

Foul—To use foot to strike ball.

Penalty—Server loses hand; receiver, point to server.

X. Hinder.—To stop a ball going to front wall, if unintentional, ball is dead and must be served again.

Foul—If intentional, hinder.

Penalty—Server loses hand; receiver, point to server.

XI. Ball to be fair must strike at least six inches above floor, that is, above the tell board.

Foul—Intentional.

Applying to doubles.

XII. Served ball strikes server's partner; called a hinder.

Foul—Hit, hinder for serving side.

Penalty—Loss of hand.

XIII. Server's partner interferes with the ball before it is played by either of the two opposing players.

Foul—Hit, hinder by server's partner.

Penalty—Loss of hand.

XIV. If a receiver strikes ball so that it strikes partner it is a hinder.

Foul—Hit, point for receiver.

XV. If a receiver strikes either of opponents with ball, a hinder.

Foul—Hit, point for receiver, decided by referee.

FENCING

How to hold the foil; on guard; parries; attack.

To some, the practice required to develop good form in fencing may at first seem tedious. This practice, however, not only rounds out the form of the fencer, but also is very beneficial in that it exercises the muscles of the entire body and in that it cultivates quick thinking and stimulates mental alertness. From the physical point of view fencing tends to develop symmetrically all the muscles of the body, to give a lightness and quickness of movement, gracefulness, and generally to strengthen the body. To fence well it is necessary to think quickly and act calmly. The fencer must judge what is best suited for her to do. She must divine her opponent's attack. Thus she must be mentally alert all the time.

For the beginner and inexperienced fencer, it is necessary to have a good foil, one that is the proper weight for the strength of the fencer. Never use a foil that is too heavy; it is better to have a light than heavy one. A foil must also have the proper balance. To test the foil lay the blade across the finger about an inch below the hilt. If the weight is properly distributed it will balance. To avoid any accidents a fine-meshed mask and plastron or jacket should always be worn. If a glove is worn it should be loose enough to allow perfect freedom of action, but not so loose as to be cumbersome.

Rubber-soled shoes or a shoe that will not slip should be worn.

How to Hold the Foil.

The handle of the foil has two sides, the concave and the convex. The foil is held, generally in the right hand, so that the concave of the handle rests in the palm; the convex is then the upper side; the fingers are closed around the handle, the thumb rests on the upper or convex side, without touching the hilt; the fingers must not overlap the thumb. The foil is held correctly when, i. e., for the right-handed fencer, the thumb nail faces upward and the finger nails toward the left. This position of the foil is called supination.

Another position is pronation. For this the back of hand is turned up, the fingers are drawn closer together and the thumb is closer to the fingers.

Form and skill count for the most in fencing, hence strict attention is paid to the different positions until the form is perfect. Quickness and good judgment are acquired with practice and experience. It is of course desirable to procure the services of a competent instructor when a beginner.

The fencer should remember to use mainly the fingers and wrist; the part played by the arms is subordinate.

Think quickly. Thrust and parry coolly and make every movement count. If your movements become hurried and flustered, the result is slashing, which is not good fencing—good headwork counts. Try to fathom your opponent's methods and take advantage of every opening she gives. Consistent practice and confidence will enable you to be ready for any situation which may come about.

On Guard.

This is the elementary position in fencing. Stand at attention, body turned facing opponent outwardly, feet at right angles, the left foot pointing forward, the right foot outward toward opponent.

1. Raise the arm holding foil lightly, extend toward opponent, hand at height of and opposite the eye.

2. Drop the arm and foil, point outward, until it is a few inches from the floor.

3. Sweep the foil across the body so that the foil is horizontal. Grasp the blade close to the guard with fingers of the left hand, palm up. The right hand is reversed.

4. Bend arms over head in a circle, carrying foil upward so it is kept horizontal.

5. Lower right hand to height of the right breast, with foil directed outward toward opponent at the height of her eyes. Drop the left elbow, curving the hand over the left shoulder.

6. Bend the legs, separating them at the knees.

7. Advance the right foot in a direct line from the left heel to opponent. The right knee should be bent over the right foot, both feet should be flat on the floor.

After these seven movements have been practised and the position on guard reached quickly and accurately, the fencer may take up more advanced work. The natural instinct is to defend oneself, so a scientific means of defense is taught. Any movement that turns away an opponent's foil is called a parry. As the fencing jacket is divided into different lines of engagement, there is a set parry for each. In all parries, it is important to turn the point of the opponent's foil away from your body. Parries are divided into two main classes, simple and counter. The following are the simple parries:

The Parry of Quarte.

Using the fingers and wrist, the foil is carried across body from right to left, turning the point of opponent's foil away from the attack; the right forearm protects the left side, the elbow is close at side and in a line with the hip bone; the tip of foil points up; the foil is held in supination.

The Parry of Sixte.

The foil moves from left to right, protecting the right side. The hand is held in supination.

The Parry of Septime.

The hand is moved as in quarte; the hand is held in supination; the point is dropped to the waistline by a semi-circular movement outward.

The Parry of Octave.

With the hand similar to that of septime the foil is moved outward in a semi-circle and the point is dropped.

Parry of Quinte.

For this, the hand from quarte is lowered toward the hip, point upward.

Parry of Tierce.

The foil is held in pronation. The parry of Sixte covers the same line of engagement except in the difference in holding the foil.

Parry of Prime.

From quarte, the hand is moved toward the left shoulder, the point dropped, the back of hand is turned upward and outward.

Parry of Seconde.

The hand is in pronation; it covers the same ground as octave.

Besides these simple parries are counter parries, which are circles described with the tip of the foil around the opponent's foil, holding the foil as close as possible to hers.

In all the parries it is practice, so that the movements are smooth and the recovery from the parry to the on-guard position is instantaneous. The fingers and wrist should be used mainly in the parries, the arm movement should be as slight as possible.

The Attack.

A fundamental of the attack first to be learned is the thrust. The tip of the foil is aimed at the point to be hit, the arm is straightened. Added to the thrust in the attack is the lunge. The right foot is carried forward (about twice its length), the left leg is straightened, the weight of the body is on the right leg, which is bent at the knee. The left arm is carried straight down at the side, palm of the hand turned outward. The thrust and the advance with the foot are simultaneous. The lunge requires much practice to develop a quick attack and recovery. One important factor to be remembered in the lunge is never to get the balance too far over the right knee. Also never let any part of the left foot leave the floor. Immediately after the lunge and the thrust, the fencer should quickly resume the original position, i. e., the on guard position.

There are many different methods of attack, divided into two main classes, primary and secondary. Primary attack is one that is begun by yourself; secondary attack is one when you attack in an opening your opponent gives in her attack. Besides these are false attacks to decoy the opponent's attack.

The Direct Lunge.—This is one form of attack, though the straight attack is generally preceded by disengages. A riposte is a thrust unaccompanied by a lunge; this is important in secondary attack.

The Disengage.—In order to attack in a center line, it may be necessary to raise the point of your foil over or drop it under the point of your adversary's.

The Counter Disengage.—This is a disengage (or more than one) followed by a circling of the tip of your foil around your opponent's foil, followed by an attack on your part.

The Coupe (cut over).—The point of the foil is raised by the fingers and carried down on the opposite side of your opponent's foil, accompanied by the lunge.

In the attack the fencer should remember to keep the right arm straight, to aim at the line carefully, to always be in a position to guard closely.

In a match or competitive bout, the umpire decides the hits, but it is courtesy to acknowledge a hit yourself.

SWIMMING

Breast stroke; side stroke; trudgeon; crawl; plain back stroke; floating; plunge for distance; diving; the racing turn; treading water; swimming meets; all-around swimming test.

A graceful swimmer is as fascinating to watch as a graceful dancer. Anyone with a thorough knowledge of the strokes and with sufficient confidence in her own ability may develop into a graceful and competent swimmer. Everyone should learn to swim well, because it is not only one of the best physical exercises, but also is a useful accomplishment in case of emergency. Swimming is an all-around exercise, since it brings into play all the muscles of the body. Not only is swimming good from the above points of view, but also as a rule it stimulates and refreshes, and combined withal there is generally an element of fun which lends zest to the sport.

Those girls who fail to enjoy their swimming do so because they have no confidence in their ability. It is foolhardy to venture into deep water when one cannot swim well, but if there are good swimmers in the proximity and a float or some other object close by which can be reached by merely stretching out the arm, then is the time to gain confidence and corresponding ability and endurance.

Never swim in dangerous water alone. Never swim when tired. Over-exertion in swimming, much more so than in other sports, should be watched for, especially in racing and long distance swims, and if any of the contestants tire, they should leave the water.

There are two faults the mediocre swimmer—even the average swimmer—is apt to have, namely, poor breathing and hurried strokes. It is important to learn to breathe well. The breathing should be regular and is varied according to the different strokes. The common tendency is to hold the breath until it is a physical impossibility to hold it any longer, then let it out through the mouth with a gasp, hold the breath again, etc.

In haste to reach the objective point, the swimmer is sometimes apt to hurry her stroke. Thereby she fails to execute her strokes in good form, usually floundering and splashing without deriving any force or impetus from her efforts. This is not only ineffectual, but it is exceedingly exhausting and tiring. The strokes should always be completed in perfect form and rhythm.

There are varied types of strokes; often one stroke is more suited to an individual than another. Swimming is just as individual as walking, for it is rarely that two people swim in identically the same manner. Often bad habits become fixed, unconsciously, even in the strokes of the best swimmers, so it is well to watch one's form carefully.

The Breast Stroke.—In the breast stroke, the swimmer is lying in the water flat upon the breast. The feet should be but a few inches below the water; the head is carried so that the mouth is just under the water; the legs are together and straight, toes pointing back; the arms are stretched straight in front, hands just touching each other, palms down, fingers together; with elbow stiff, the arms are circled back close under and parallel to the surface until they are at right angles to the body; the hands are turned in the beginning of the stroke so that the palms are outward; then the elbows are bent so that they are drawn back and close to the body, and the hands, palms down, are brought together at the chest, ready to shoot forward to the starting position; when the arms are drawn back the mouth is carried above the water, then the swimmer should inhale through the mouth; when the arms shoot forward then exhale, preferably through the nostrils; the beginning of the kick is made as the arms are drawn up to the chest; the legs are drawn up, heels together, knees bent out; simultaneously as the hands are shot forward, legs are kicked outward, then the heels are brought quickly together.

In this stroke the body gets its impetus from the reach of the arms and the kick. Thus the body should glide through the water until the momentum is used up, then the arms are circled back, etc. Always try to utilize the momentum. All the parts of the stroke quickly follow one another, so that the entire stroke is smooth.

The Side Stroke.—In this stroke the kick is very important. The scissors kick is used. The body lies with shoulder and side flat in the water, usually the right side; the upper leg is kept straight, almost stiff, and is kicked forward; the under leg is bent backward from the knee; then the legs are brought together and closed with a snap; the arms are stretched overhead, palms out; the upper arm, kept rigid, with the hand slightly cupped, circles just under the surface to the thigh, then the elbow is bent and the arm carried above the water to the first position; the under arm starts as the upper finishes and is carried to lower thigh; then, the elbow bent, it is shot forward *under* the surface of the water, palm of hand down.

The whole stroke is: Upper arm starts the pull, the legs are opened, and breath is inhaled; then as the upper arm finishes the under arm starts, the legs are snapped together; breath is exhaled as the under arm goes forward.

The Trudgeon.—The scissors kick as described in the side stroke is used also in the trudgeon. This kick is very important and should be practised carefully until the swimmer is perfect.

It is always better to swim on the right side if it is possible, as it relieves the pressure the heart is apt to be subjected to if the swimmer prefers the left side. The body rests in the water, arm stretched at full length, the palms are turned down; the upper arm catches the water and is brought down, the elbow is fairly stiff, palms turned slightly outward, fingers together; when arm is straight alongside the body, then the elbow is bent and the arm carried forward above the water to the first position; as the upper arm finishes, the under arm executes the same stroke as the upper arm; the body is rolled.

The whole stroke should be practised together, so that it is smoothly and accurately done. First, the upper arm catches the water, the body is slightly rolled, head twisted so that breath may be inhaled during the pull, the legs are opened at start of pull and closed at the end of pull. Then under arm catches the water, the body is rolled so that the face is in the water, and during the pull the breath is exhaled slowly under the water. Then, as under arm finishes the pull, the upper arm enters the water, etc.

The Crawl.—The crawl is the racing stroke. The best-way to begin is first to perfect the movement of the arms. The body is flat in the water, face down, arms slightly bent at the elbow, stretched over head so that wrists are a little beyond the head; the hands cut and are driven through the water, elbows still bent, until the hands reach the hip, then they are carried out the water and forward, elbows in air. The arms alternate, so that while one arm is traveling back under the water, the other is traveling forward in the air to resume the stroke.

The breathing in this stroke is hard to master. As the face is in the water, the breath is taken only every two or three strokes by turning the head quickly as the upper arm is being brought down; the exhaling is done under water, while the under arm goes forward. This is for racing; a breath may be taken at each stroke when the stroke is slower.

In the kick, the legs are stiff from the hip, knees close together, then they are moved up and down alternately with the feet close together. It is difficult at first to maintain the leg drive, to make the whole stroke smooth, and to breathe easily, but these difficulties may be conquered by practice.

Plain Back Stroke.—The body is flat on the back in the water, the arms are straight over the head, the palms of hands upward; the palms are turned outward, then the arms, stiff at the elbow, are circled down close to the surface and parallel to it; after the arms are straight by the body, they are carried to the first position, perfectly straight, and clear of the water; the legs are straight, then as the arms clear the water for the recovery, they are bent as in the breast stroke kick, kicked out straight, then the heels are brought together.

This stroke is almost the same as the breast stroke.

Another stroke is the same positions for the arms as the plain back stroke combined with the leg drive of the crawl.

Still another is the same, except that the arms move alternately as in trudgeon stroke.

Floating.—In order to float on the back, the balance of the body must be determined; hence it is often necessary if the feet sink to throw the head back and raise the arms over the head. In some cases, if the legs are bent, it helps the balance. After practice, the swimmer soon learns to float. Short breaths, keeping the lungs as full of air as possible, are better than long ones.

Plunge for Distance.—In reality this is floating with the face flat down in the water. The first part of the plunge is the dive, which gives the impetus. The dive taken is the shallow dive. As the breath is held from the minute the head enters the water until the plunge is finished, it is necessary that the lungs be well filled. After the body is in the water, the muscles should be relaxed, and the swimmer should keep the air in the lower part of the lungs. The plunge should be as straight as possible; the direction may be changed by moving the arms (which are stretched straight out in front) or the head in the direction desired. This motion should be slight, as the least friction impedes progress, and distance is the desired result.

DIVING.

As diving is a very large subject, it is impossible to give in detail all the varied dives. There are three important dives everyone should know—the front, back, and shallow or racing dive. The beauty of diving is in the form.

The Front Dive.—The diver stands erect at the end of the spring board, falls forward, then as the body passes the balance point, the arms are raised straight over the head, knees bent; then spring out so that the body is parallel to water, arms above head; the body is curved downward and enters the water, arms, head, body, and legs forming a straight line.

In springing, jump out parallel to the water. The running dive is very similar.

Back Dive.—The diver turns with back to the water, heels over the edge of board into space; the arms are over head, body is curved backward; as the balance point is reached, spring out, turning body as it enters the water.

The position of the head is important. Ducking the head or throwing it too far back, added to stiffness of the body, makes the dive awkward. The legs should never be apart, but together; toes pointed, so that feet are not flat; the fingers should be together.

The shallow dive, known as the racing dive, is important for those interested in speed swimming, as is the racing turn.

The Racing Dive.—The swimmer stands with the body bent forward, arms back; then, as body falls forward, the knees are bent and the spring out is taken; the body strikes the water arms over head, the whole body in a straight line with the arms and legs. Do not dive so that you sink into the water, but try to strike it at the right angle, so that you will sink only a few inches. The arms start the stroke as soon as they reach the surface, then the legs commence as the arms are recovering.

The Racing Turn.—The wall is touched by the arm that the turn is to be made on. The previous strokes must be timed so that the arm may touch the wall stretched straight out in front. The hand touches the wall (above the water line) palm against the wall, fingers pointing the way the body is to turn.

The body is swung along the wall so that bottoms of the feet touch the wall (a little below the water); then with a backward stroke of the arms, which have been brought to the hip, palms pointing in front, fingers down, the body is brought right against the wall, nearly touching; then the arms are forward, the legs straightened, thus gaining impetus; the arms start the stroke, then the legs commence as the arms start the recovery.

For racing, constant practice of the start, stroke and turn is necessary. First the swimmer should perfect her form of stroke, then the speed may be increased by practice swims of a short distance at first, which may be increased slowly. A swimmer should always be in good condition. Never swim so much as to get stale; never over-exert. It doesn't pay in the end.

Choose the event you are the most proficient in and stick to that one until you are perfect in it.

Treading Water.

It is necessary for the water polo player to know how to tread water, that is, to remain stationary in the water with the least effort. The body is upright in the water, as in a standing position. The legs are moved up and down, the arms are spread out, bent at the elbow, and moved up and down gently. The whole movement should be as slight as possible, so that the greatest possible amount of rest may be obtained.

Swimming Meets.

For swimming meets there should be a set program of events. The contestants should be entered ahead of time. Handicaps may be granted if the swimmers are unevenly matched.

There should be a referee to conduct the meet; a clerk of the course, who sees that the participants are notified of the events; a scorer, who keeps an official score; three judges, who watch for fouls; three timers, a starter, and an announcer.

Score.—The score is, as a rule, 5 for first place, 3 for second, 1 for third. Relay races are often counted in different ways: 5 points, 6 points, or 8 points are the most common for the first place.

The signal for the start should be: 1. "Get- on your marks." 2. "Get set." 3. "Go." (Pistol shot.) There should be no stepping over or back from starting line.

Three false starts disqualify a competitor.

Each swimmer should keep in her own course. If she crosses into the course of another swimmer and touches her she is liable to disqualification.

In turning the swimmer should touch the end of the pool with one or both hands.

The swimmer must touch the finish line with a hand out of the water.

If the stroke is judged for form the competitor must dive into the water, swim a given distance, turn, all in perfect form.

In the plunge for distance the dive should be made from a firm take-off. The body must be kept motionless, face down, no longer than sixty seconds, however. The distance is measured from a line parallel to the diving base, at right angles to base, to the farthest point reached by any part of the body.

A certain number of plunges, usually two or three, is allowed to each competitor.

In diving there are usually a list of required and voluntary dives. The judges consider the form with which the dive was executed. (Form is treated under diving.) The scale of points usually is:

Unsuccessful attempt, 0; Poor dive, 3; Fair dive, 6; Good dive, 8; Excellent dive, 10.

Swimming Test.

The all-around swimming test as practised at Bryn Mawr College in a 68-foot pool, the details of which have been contributed by Mr. Philip Bishop, Athletic Director of the Haverford School and Advisory Swimming Coach at Bryn Mawr College, is given herewith.

All-Around Swimming Test for Women

By Philip Bishop.

This test is taken in three sections: diving, plunge and object dive in one section; form and speed in another; endurance and underwater swim in the third.

Section 1.—Speed test, two lengths to be done in 44 seconds; form swimming, breast stroke, back stroke and trudgeon, or crawl stroke.

Section 2.—Endurance test, 150 yards in 3 minutes; underwater swim, 50 feet.

Section 3.—Diving, standing straight dive, running straight dive, standing high dive; fancy diving, four dives, which include jackknife, back dive and somersaults; plunge, 30 feet; object dive, must pick up 6 rings in 3 attempts.

The successful competitor must score 85 per cent to qualify as a first-class swimmer.

This test is by no means a hard one, but it requires practice. The object is to make all-around swimmers and to teach the correct method of diving and making the strokes employed.

WATER BASKET BALL AND WATER POLO

Water Basket Ball—The game and rules.

Water Polo—The game; rules.

Water basket ball and water polo are two thrilling and interesting games. They are so similar in general characteristics that they are treated here in the same chapter.

From my own experience I believe them to be the most strenuous games played by women. By that I do not mean that they are necessarily harmful. I do believe, however, that they should be played only under the most careful supervision of a medical or physical training authority. Two points should be considered before a girl is permitted to participate in either of these games:

1. All players should be in perfect physical condition.

2. All players should be strong and capable swimmers.

3. Careful examination should be made of each player when she comes from the tank at the end of the first period and after the game, for that, after all, is the best test as to whether she is fit.

1. To be in good condition the player should have perfect heart action and good lung capacity, and she should be generally in good condition.

2. She should be a swimmer of endurance, experience and confidence. The beginner tires in the effort to swim strongly and constantly.

3. If the player is qualified in every respect she may try the game. If after playing she seems exhausted or chilled, and is tired the following day, then she has not the stamina to participate in water sports.

Water Basket Ball.

[Reprinted from Spalding's Athletic Library No. 361—Intercollegiate Swimming Guide.]

Water basket ball may be played in any pool, or if played in the open should not cover more than 2,500 square feet of space. The water should be of swimming depth, that is, the players must not be able to stand on the bottom. There should be lines drawn "across the bottom of the pool and up the sides 15 feet from the ends, called 15-foot lines."

Equipment.—The necessary equipment is a regulation water polo ball and two regulation Spalding baskets with a firm background, 6 feet by 4, extending at least 3 feet above the top of each basket. The baskets shall be hammock nets of cord, suspended from metal rings 18 inches in diameter. The rings shall be 5½ feet above the water in the center of the ends of the pool. The inside rims shall extend 6 inches from a rigid supporting surface.

Teams.—Each team consists of six players-three forwards and three backs. Captains toss for goals.

Start.—Each team lines up at its own end; the ball is thrown into center of the pool; the forwards swim after the ball; the backs must play back and not swim up after ball. The forwards are the offensive players and should be the fastest swimmers. They should also be able to throw goals. The forwards advance the ball toward the opponents' basket. The center forward should feed the two side forwards and guard the opposing center back.

Score.—A goal thrown into the basket from the field counts two points, and a free throw granted for a foul by opposing side counts one point. Teams line up as in beginning after a score has been made. The backs each guard an opposing forward and try to prevent their scoring.

Officials.—There is a referee who is in entire charge of game, calling fouls, free throws, time out and goals. There is a scorer, also a timer.

Time.—There are two halves, not less than five minutes nor more than eight minutes each, with five minutes intermission. Ends are changed at the beginning of the second half. Time is taken out for disputes, accidents, free tries.

Out of Bounds.—When the ball is sent out of bounds by one team it is given to a player of opposing team at place where it went out. Player must throw ball within five seconds or it is given to opposing side.

Free Throw.—A free throw is granted to a forward upon a foul made by opposite side. The free throw is taken from the fifteen-foot mark by one of the forwards, who is unguarded at time of throw. If the goal is not made, the ball is in play. If goal is made, play begins according to start.

Fouls.—The penalty for a foul is a free throw for opposing side. There are rough fouls such as kicking, striking, tackling, holding, deliberate splashings.

When an opponent has the ball she may be tackled and "ducked" under the water by one of the opposing players.

A player may not be held under water after she has let go of ball. A player may not tackle by or hold to opponent's clothing, although blocking is allowed. There should be no holding with hands or legs. A player may not hang on to sides when she has the ball. The ball may not intentionally be held under water.

Tie.—A tie may be played off in another three-minute period. If game ends after foul is made, the free throw is taken. No goal is counted after whistle has blown.

In both water basket ball and water polo the swimmer should use the easiest and least tiring stroke. Whenever there is an opportunity, a rest either by hanging on to sides or treading water (see Swimming) ought to be taken. Both games afford opportunity for team work in passing and dribbling. In dribbling, the ball is kept in front of body within easy reach for a good pass if the dribbler is attacked.

Water Polo.

The main factor in water polo is learning how to handle the ball. The hand should be placed under the ball, then the ball is lifted in the air and thrown with all the strength of the shoulder and arm. It is ineffectual to try to grab the ball or push it. It must be picked up.

The ball is tossed to the middle of the pool, then the forwards swim up as fast as they can to get the ball. The forwards are chosen for their speed and endurance. Every forward should learn to shoot hard and accurately. The center forward is usually the fastest girl on the team. The center forward who gets the ball in the swim-up usually tosses it back to her center-half or to one of the side forwards. The forwards try to advance the ball, so that a good shot for their opponents' goal may be obtained. If the field is clear the forward may dribble the ball, i. e., keep the ball moving close in front of her. Usually, however, it is better to advance the ball by passes. One forward at least should stay close to the goal, ready to send in any short shots.

The center half guards the opposing forward and feeds the ball to her forwards. There is a guard for each of the side forwards. It is the best policy for the guards to stay between the forwards and the goal. Stick to your opponent; never let her get a free shot.

The goal keeper must be able to reach out of the water and catch the high balls sent into the goal. She must also be quick. Remember, you can use both hands to handle the ball. The guards always must help the goal keeper cover the goal area, never leaving her unguarded, yet they must not interfere with her or prevent her seeing clearly.

Water Polo Rules.

[Printed through courtesy of Mr. Philip Bishop, Physical Director Haverford School and Advisory Coach of Swimming at Bryn Mawr College.]

Ball.—The ball used shall be a leather association football.

Goals.—The width of the goals to be 10 feet, the cross-bar to be 3 feet above the surface when the water is 5 feet or over in depth, and to be 8 feet from the bottom when the water is less than 5 feet in depth.

Field of Play.—The distance between the goals shall not exceed 30 yards, nor be less than 19 yards; the width shall be not more than 20 yards and shall be of even width throughout the field of play. The goal posts shall be fixed at least 1 foot from the end of the bath or any obstruction. In baths, the halfway line and also the 4 yards penalty lines shall be marked on both sides.

What greater pleasure can anyone enjoy during the summer than a good swim in the open. The picture shows the girls of the New York Public Schools Athletic League practising diving in one of their pools.

Volley Ball—a comparatively new game. It is splendid for growing school girls and may be played in recess periods—exciting, exhilarating, healthful.

Time.—The duration of the match shall be 14 minutes, 7 minutes each way. Three minutes to be allowed at half time for change of ends. When the ball crosses the goal line, whether it be a goal, corner throw or goal throw, it shall be dead until the restart of the game or until it leaves the hand of the player taking the throw, and such time shall be deducted. Time occupied by disputes and fouls, or when the ball is thrown from the field of play or lodges on an obstruction, as per Rule for Out of Play, shall not be reckoned as in time of play.

Officials.—The officials shall consist of a referee, a timekeeper, two goal scorers and two umpires.

Teams.—Each side shall consist of seven players, two forwards, two halves, two fullbacks and one goal keeper.

Starting.—The players shall enter the water and place themselves in a line with their respective goals. The referee shall stand in a line with the center of the course and, having ascertained that the captains are ready, shall give the word "Go," and immediately throw the ball into the water at the center. A goal shall not be scored after starting or restarting until the ball has been handled (viz., played with the hand below the wrist) either by the members of one team, in which case the scorer shall be within half-distance of the goal attacked, or by a player of each team. The ball must be handled by more than one player before a goal can be scored.

Scoring.—A goal shall be scored by the entire ball passing beyond the goal posts and under the cross-bar.

Ordinary Fouls.—It shall be a foul:

(*a*) To touch the ball with both hands at the same time.

(*b*) To hold the rail or side during any part of the game, except for rest. Goal keeper cannot interfere while holding, but can hold all the time so long as she does not play.

(*c*) To stand or touch bottom during any part of the game, except for the purpose of resting.

(*d*) To interfere with an opponent or impede her in any way unless she is holding the ball.

(*e*) To hold the ball under water when tackled.

(*f*) To jump from the bottom or push off from the side (except at starting or restarting) in order to play the ball or "duck" an opponent.

(*g*) To hold, pull back, or push off from an opponent.

(*h*) To turn on the back and kick at an opponent.

(*i*) To assist a player at the start or restart.

(*j*) For the goal keeper to go more than 4 yards from her own goal lines.

(*k*) To throw the ball at the goal keeper from a free throw.

(*l*) To refuse to play the ball at the command of the referee after a foul or after the ball has been out of the field of play.

Note.—Dribbling or striking the ball is not holding; but lifting, carrying, pressing under water or placing the hand under or over the ball when actually touching, is holding. Dribbling the ball lip through the posts is permissible.

Wilful Fouls.—If, in the opinion of the referee, a player commits an ordinary foul wilfully, the referee shall at once order her out of the water until a goal has been scored. It shall be considered a wilful foul to start before word "go;" to deliberately waste time; to deliberately change position after whistle has blown with a view to taking an advantage of an opponent; to deliberately splash in the face of an opponent.

Free Throws.—The penalty for each foul shall be a free throw to the opposing side from the place where the foul occurred. A goal cannot be scored from a free throw, unless the ball has been handled (viz., played with the hand below the wrist), by at least one other player, the goal keeper excepted.

Penalty Throws.—A player wilfully fouled when within four yards of her opponents' goal line shall be awarded a penalty throw, and the player who commits the offense must be ordered out of the water until a goal has been scored. The penalty throw shall be taken from any point on the four-yard line. In the case of a penalty throw it shall not be necessary for the ball to be handled by any other player before the goal can be scored, but any player within the four-yard line may intercept a penalty throw.

Note.—A player ordered out of the water for committing a wilful foul must remain out until a goal has been scored, notwithstanding that half-time may intervene or extra time be played, except by permission of the referee.

Declaring Fouls.—The referee or umpires shall declare a foul by blowing a whistle. The player nearest to where the foul occurred shall take the throw. The other players shall remain in their respective positions from the blowing of the whistle until the ball has left the hand of the player taking the throw. In the event of one or more players from each team committing a foul so nearly at the same moment as to make it impossible for the referee to distinguish who offended first, she shall have the ball out of the water and throw it in as nearly as possible at the place where the foul occurred in such a manner that one member of each team may have equal chance of playing the ball. In such cases the ball must be allowed to touch the water before it is handled and must be handled (i. e., played with the hand below the wrist) by more than one player before a goal can be scored.

Goal Keeper.—The goal keeper may stand to defend her goal, and must not throw the ball beyond half distance; the penalty for doing so shall be a free throw to the opposing side from half distance at either side of the field of play. She must keep within four yards of her own goal line or concede a free throw from the four-yard line to her nearest opponent. The goal keeper is exempt from clauses *a, c,* and *f* in Rule for Ordinary Fouls, but she may be treated as any other player when in possession of the ball. Except when injury or illness compel her to leave the water, the goal keeper can only be changed at half time.

Goal Line Corner Throws.—A player throwing the ball over her own goal line shall concede a free corner throw to her opponents, and such free corner throw shall be taken by the player of the opposing side nearest the point where the ball leaves the field of play; if the attacking side throw the ball over, it shall be a free goal throw to their opponents' goal keeper.

Out of Play.—Should a player send the ball out of the field of play at either side, it shall be thrown in any direction from where it went out by one of the opposing side, and shall be considered a free throw. The player nearest the point where the ball leaves the field of play must take the throw. Should a ball strike an overhead obstruction and rebound into the field of play, it shall be considered in play; but if it lodges on or in an overhead obstruction, it shall be considered out of play, and the referee shall then stop the game and throw the ball into the water under the obstruction on or in which it had lodged.

Declaring Goals, Time, etc.—The referee shall declare fouls, half-time and time by whistle; the timekeeper may notify half-time and time by whistle.

VOLLEY BALL

Volley ball is another team game which is rapidly becoming popular among girls. It may be played indoors or outdoors and can be enjoyed by large groups of girls. The game is a combination of tennis and hand ball and consists of keeping a ball in motion over a high net.

Many girls, particularly the young and those who are weakly, are compelled to refrain from indulging in many of our most popular games. These can play volley ball without running the risk of any serious injury. There is no bodily contact with opponents. The ball is soft and does not injure the one hitting it or anyone who may accidentally be hit with it.

The space, ball and net usually can be acquired with little difficulty, and the ball and net are very inexpensive when we consider how long they last and the number of games which can be enjoyed by a great many persons before they have to be repaired or replaced.

While the rules call for a definite size of court, it should be remembered that a good game can be played and lots of fun enjoyed in school rooms and other places that may be available, where the space and other requirements are less than those specified.

The rules for the game are revised annually by a joint committee of the Young Men's Christian Association and the National Collegiate Athletic Association and are published in Spalding's Athletic Library.

PHILADELPHIA HOCKEY LEAGUE

BY JOSEPHINE KATZENSTEIN.

[The Philadelphia Hockey League has been successfully organized as is told by Miss Josephine Katzenstein, a member of the Lansdowne hockey team. Miss Katzenstein has been chosen for the All-Philadelphia team every year since its start. Previous to this, she played on the Bryn Mawr 'varsity. It is needless to say that she is one of the best forwards that ever played in the Philadelphia League.—EDITOR.]

When we consider that before 1901 field hockey for women was hardly more than a name in and around Philadelphia, and that since that year enthusiasm for the game has so steadily grown that we have now perhaps the finest hockey league in the country, we may justly feel optimistic on the subject of athletics for women.

In 1907, there were eight hockey clubs in this vicinity—enough to organize an inter-club hockey league. Merion Cricket Club, Belmont Cricket Club, Lansdowne Country Club, Germantown Hockey Club, Philadelphia Cricket Club, Moorestown Field Club, Haddonfield Hockey Club, and Frankford Cricket Club composed the league. Later Belmont went out of existence, Frankford and Moorestown withdrew, and Temple College joined the league. Now Lansdowne, Germantown, Haddonfield, Philadelphia and Merion have second teams, while Riverton plays only in the second league.

The different teams must have distinguishing colors, and no club joining the league may use the colors already adopted by another club. So far Temple is the only club far-sighted enough to play in bloomers instead of in hampering skirts. It is hoped by many that all may soon follow her wise example. Professionals are barred from competition on any league team. A team may be admitted to the league upon application to and approval by the Executive Committee. Each team has to play two matches with every other club in the league—one on the home field and one on the opponent's.

Since 1908 a committee formed of a representative from each club has chosen an All-Philadelphia team to play outside teams, after the inter-club games are over. This has proved an incentive to consistently good playing all season, as one knows that the critics' eyes are on one in every game. It has also helped to spread the interest in hockey.

Bryn Mawr, New York, Baltimore and Rosemary Hall (Greenwich, Conn.) teams have been met repeatedly by the All-Philadelphia team.

ACTIVITY OF MISSOURI COLLEGES

BY MISS LORENA L. PARRISH,

Physical Director Howard Payne College.

It is with pleasure that I take this opportunity to give you a glimpse of the work of the Junior Colleges of Missouri in Athletics.

In 1914, the organization known as the Junior College Athletic Association of Missouri was formed. Up until this time there were only a few of the colleges devoting much time to athletics. Howard Payne has for years been one of the strongest supporters of athletics for women, not only within her own college, but a strong advocate of intercollegiate sports. Since the organization there have been four out of the seven junior colleges which have taken up active intercollegiate basket ball-Christian College and Stephens College, both of Columbia, Mo., Lindenwood of St. Charles and Howard Payne of Fayette. I feel confident that in another year the remaining three will join our ranks. We also have our tennis tournaments every spring.

In the year 1915, we started for the first time work in track and field athletics. A dual meet was held here on May 17 between Howard Payne and Stephens. It met with such overwhelming success that we have planned to make it an annual event. There were several physicians present at the meet, and they were very enthusiastic in their praise of the work, saying that it was one of the finest moves that had been made within recent years for the development of our girls. Notwithstanding these facts, there is still a great deal of prejudice against this particular form of athletics, and the two questions that are uppermost in the minds of a great many are: "Are we taking chances with the girls' future health by allowing these sports?" "Do the advantages gained overshadow the possible danger?" These questions should be given careful consideration by the physical directors and they should see to it that the girls under their charge receive careful training and supervision. It is only in this way that we shall be able to break down the prevailing prejudices. I should say that under proper conditions and supervision the gain in health and strength far outweighs the risks of danger. Here in our own school the girls who are most active in athletics are the healthiest and are rarely ever absent from classes because of illness.

Since the meet held here in Fayette in 1915 was the first intercollegiate meet of its kind for girls in this section of the country, it might be of interest to include in this article the various events used:

Target shooting
50-yard dash
Base ball throw
60-yard hurdles (3 hurdles)
Discus—2 ½ pounds
75-yard dash
Shot-put—8 pounds
Running high jump
Basket ball throw
Running broad jump
220-yard dash

GIRLS' BRANCH OF THE PUBLIC SCHOOLS ATHLETIC LEAGUE

Among the sanctioned activities of the Girls' Branch of the Public Schools Athletic League are the following team games for the Elementary Schools: End Ball, Captain Ball, Basket Ball, Punch Ball, Indoor Base Ball.

End Ball can be played by a varied number of players. The playing rules are to be found in the Official Handbook of the Girls' Branch of the Public Schools Athletic League, published by the American Sports Publishing Company. This book says: "The object of the game is for the guards on one side to throw the ball over the heads of the guards on the opposite side to their own basemen, at the end of the opposite field. Each such ball caught by a baseman shall score one point for the side catching it.

"The object of the intervening guards is to intercept the ball before it can reach the basemen at their rear, and to throw it in turn to their own basemen at the rear of the opposite court, over the heads of the intervening opponents."

Captain Ball.—"The main object of the game is for the basemen of a team to pass the ball from one to another, each pass successfully made scoring for the team, as described under 'Score.'

"The object of the guards is to intercept the passage of the ball and send it back to their own basemen for similar play." For the rules and details see Official Handbook of the League.

Basket Ball.—The Spalding Athletic Library rules for the line game are used.

Punch Ball.—For this the league rules as set forth in Official Handbook. "The object of the batter is to hit the ball into the field in such a way that it may not be caught by the fielders, and to run to first base. The object of the fielders is to return the ball to their catcher, who shall stand on the home plate and hold the ball before the batter reaches first base. If the fielders muff the ball and are slow in returning it to home plate, the batter who has reached first may continue on to second or third base, or as far as in her judgement she can get before the ball reaches home plate. The player running the bases may always advance a base whenever the opportunity occurs and the ball is in play. The final object of the player running to the bases is to touch each base and to reach the home plate without being put out, thus scoring one run for her side."

Besides these team games, the league sanctions the following activities, which are conducted according to rules and regulations set forth in the Official Handbook: Folk Dancing, Walking, Swimming, Horseback Riding, Ice and Roller Skating, Rope Skipping, Bicycling, Coasting, Golf, Lawn Tennis, Hand Tennis, Heavy Gymnastics, Track and Field Events, Field Hockey, Volley Ball, Newcomb and Pin Ball.

INTERCOLLEGIATE ALUMNAE ATHLETIC ASSOCIATION

BY MISS LILLIAN SCHOEDLER,

Originator and Honorary President of the Intercollegiate A. A. A.; Chairman of the Alumnae Committee on Athletics of Barnard College.

New York witnessed the establishment of the first Intercollegiate Alumnæ Athletic Association the world has known. And its organization proves beyond a doubt the strong grip that athletics are getting on the modern woman.

In 1913 a group of twenty-five alumnæ from Barnard College, which met for swimming and basket ball, sowed the seed for the present association. That seed grew so quickly that by 1916 there had been 974 enrollments for the athletic work which the Alumnae Committee on Athletics of Barnard College had originated, and the activities had grown until they included, besides basket ball and swimming, social, folk and æsthetic dancing, bowling, hand ball, gymnasium work, indoor and outdoor horseback riding, with drill work, polo and basket ball on horseback, field hockey, base ball, tennis, tramping, summer boat and trolley trips, swimming parties, and college picnics of all kinds.

Three factors have contributed to the success of the alumnæ athletic movement in New York. In the first place, its activities have been carried on outside of business hours—in evenings, or during week-ends—so that college women who work, as well as their more leisurely sisters, could enjoy the fun. In the second place, the social end as well as the athletic has been provided for in the making of all plans, and as a result alumnæ athletics, through their informality and atmosphere of "camaraderie," are serving to bring together college individuals and groups as nothing else can. And, in the third place, everything has been planned as simply and inexpensively as possible, as witness the fact that horses are secured at one of the best New York academies for sixty-three cents an hour, including instruction, and that members who have no habits ride in middy blouses and bloomers. There is no pretense at "style," but every emphasis on fun.

The new association is a pioneer in its field, and is being watched with much interest by college men and women alike. It is hoped that before long similar associations will spring up in various sections of the country, and that college women will soon have the organized facilities for exercise and recreation for the possession of which they have always envied their college brothers.

Which city will be the first to follow New York's successful example?

* * * * *

Miss Schoedler has very kindly consented to give advice to any group of college women in any city who wish to form an organization for the purpose of continuing athletics. Communications to Miss Schoedler at 249 West 107th Street, New York City, will result in a prompt answer.—The Editor.

9 789361 380341

Printed by Libri Plureos GmbH in Hamburg, Germany